BUT THEY
DIDN'T
READ ME
MY RIGHTS!

BUT THEY DIDN'T READ ME MY RIGHTS!

MYTHS,

ODDITIES,

AND LIES

ABOUT OUR

LEGAL SYSTEM

MICHAEL D. CICCHINI, JD & AMY B. KUSHNER, PHD

Prometheus Books

59 John Glenn Drive
Amherst, New York 14228–2119

Published 2010 by Prometheus Books

Inquiries should be addressed to
Prometheus Books
59 John Glenn Drive
Amherst, New York 14228–2119
VOICE: 716–691–0133
FAX: 716–691–0137
WWW.PROMETHEUSBOOKS.COM

14 13 12 11 10   5 4 3 2 1

Library of Congress Cataloging-in-Publication Data

Cicchini, Michael D., 1967–
    But they didn't read me my rights! : myths, oddities, and lies about our legal system/ By Michael D. Cicchini and Amy B. Kushner.
        p. cm.
    Includes bibliographical references and index.
    ISBN 978–1–61614–166–0 (pbk.)
    1. Law—United States—Popular works. I. Kushner, Amy B., 1971–

KF387 .C39 2010
349.73—dc22
                                                            2009050902

Printed in the United States of America

Dedications

Michael Cicchini dedicates this book to his father, Dave Cicchini, and to the memory of his mother, Clare Cicchini.

Amy Kushner dedicates this book to her parents, Gail and Ralph Kushner, for their unwavering love and support; to Jay McRoy, for being one of "the two of them"; and to Chip and Sarah, for completing the family.

Both authors dedicate this book to Sarvan Singh, who, in a moment of brilliance, suggested that they write this book.

Contents

Introduction   13

DISCLAIMER—READ THIS FIRST!   17

Acknowledgments   19

THAT'S A CRIME?

1   Is it against the law to look at someone
    the wrong way?   23
2   Can you be convicted of drunk driving
    if you're not driving the car?   26
3   Can a professional fighter be charged with battery
    for winning a fight?   29
4   Is marijuana legal?   32
5   Can you be convicted of bail jumping if you
    never leave the state?   34
6   Can you be convicted of a crime for yelling
    in your own home?   37
7   Can you be convicted of
    "carrying a concealed weapon"
    if your gun is *not* concealed?   41

SEX CRIMES

8   Can you be convicted of "statutory rape"
    if the minor lied about his or her age?   47
9   Is oral sex illegal?   50
10   Is it a crime to cheat on your spouse?   53
11   Is prostitution legal in Las Vegas?   56

PROBLEMS WITH THE POLICE

12   Do the police have to read you your rights
     when they arrest you?   61
13   Can the police search your car if you have
     an air freshener hanging on the mirror?   65
14   Can the police tell when you are lying?   69
15   Can the police lie to you when they interrogate you?   73
16   Can the police search your home without a warrant?   77
17   Can you make a citizen's arrest?   81

CRIMINAL PROCESS AND PROCEDURE

18   Since I'm innocent until proven guilty,
     will I still have to sit in jail before trial?   87
19   Can a child be convicted of a crime?   90
20   If you accuse someone of a crime,
     can you later "drop the charges"?   93
21   If you punch someone in a fight,
     are your hands considered dangerous weapons?   97

YOUR DAY IN CRIMINAL COURT

22   Can hearsay be used against you in court?   103
23   Does a speedy trial mean you'll get your trial
     within six months?   107

24 Can you be convicted of a crime for a mistake
    or an accident?   110
25 Can you be convicted of multiple crimes
    for a single act?   115
26 Can you be convicted of a crime without
    any evidence?   118
27 If a jury convicts you of a crime,
    can you appeal the verdict?   121
28 Can you beat your case by claiming you're insane?   125
29 If you're charged with a crime,
    can you represent yourself in court?   129

FIRST KILL ALL THE LAWYERS

30 Are public defenders "real lawyers"?   135
31 If you can't afford a lawyer,
    will the court appoint one for you?   139

CONTRACT LAW: A DEAL IS A DEAL

32 Do contracts have to be in writing to be enforceable? 147
33 Will a contract be enforceable *because*
    it is in writing?   150
34 Can promises be enforced,
    even if they're not enforceable as contracts?   153
35 Can a minor (under eighteen years old)
    enter into a contract?   156
36 Are disclaimers, or no-liability clauses, enforceable? 160
37 Are there legal ways to get out of
    an otherwise enforceable contract?   164

FAMILY LAW: LOVE AND MARRIAGE

38   If you break up with your fiancé,
     can you keep the ring?   171
39   In a divorce, does the mother have an advantage
     over the father for child custody?   174
40   In a divorce, can a "pre-nup" protect your assets
     from your ex-spouse?   177
41   Can the government order you to pay support
     for someone else's child?   181

TAXES: CUZ I'M THE TAXMAN

42   If you find lost or abandoned property,
     do you have to pay taxes on it?   187
43   If you barter for goods or services,
     do you have to pay taxes?   190

REAL PROPERTY LAW: I KNOW WHAT'S MINE

44   Is it possible to lose your property through
     "adverse possession"?   195
45   Is it possible to use your neighbor's property
     without trespassing?   198

TORTS: SUE HAPPY

46   Can you sue a restaurant if your coffee is too hot?   203
47   Can a burglar sue me if he gets injured
     on my property?   207
48   Can I be sued for helping someone
     during an emergency?   210
49   People are spreading rumors about me—
     can I sue them for slander?   214

LEGAL EDUCATION: SO YOU WANT TO BE A LAWYER?

50   Do you have to go to law school to be a lawyer?   219
51   Do you have to pass the bar exam to be a lawyer?   222
52   Do all lawyers go to trial?   225
53   Is becoming a lawyer the road to riches?   228

Afterword   233

Endnotes   235

Index   273

About the Authors   275

Introduction

Why should you read this book?

Because you are someone who is very interested in and recognizes the reach and importance of American law. We're not talking about simple legal factoids, such as "the United States incarcerates more people than any other nation in the world." Nor are we talking about strange or bizarre laws that don't really affect anyone, such as "it is illegal to have a slug as a pet in the state of California." Factoids and strange laws may sometimes be mildly entertaining, but you're looking for something a bit more substantive.

What you're interested in are real laws and, more important, how they might affect people in their real lives. For example, do the police have to read you your rights before they arrest you? Can you be convicted of drunk driving if you weren't even driving the car? Can the police search your home without a warrant? Can hearsay evidence be used against you in court? Do contracts have to be written to be enforceable? If you break up with your fiancé, can you keep the ring? Do you have to go to law school and pass the bar exam to become a lawyer?

These and other questions about real laws and their impact on real people will be answered in this book. And while American law is complex, which usually prevents a simple yes or no answer, this book will answer the questions as clearly and succinctly as possible, without using any legalese or lawyer jargon to complicate matters. This book will also tell you *why* the answer is what it is, and what facts or circumstances, if different, would change the answer.

When reading this book, we think you'll be entertained and often surprised. What you'll probably discover is that many of the things you thought you knew about the law are nothing more than legal myths or misconceptions. Our goal is not only to clear up misperceptions but also to provide you with some insight into the process of legal reasoning in American law. This new insight will enable you to question and criticize other laws with which you'll likely come into contact long after reading this book. After all, law is all around us and affects nearly every area of our lives. For that reason, laws cannot be memorized; there are simply too many of them and, on top of that, they change all the time. That's why the process of legal reasoning is so important.

Each chapter in this book deals with a distinct legal issue. While some chapters certainly incorporate concepts from other chapters, we did our best to make each chapter self-contained. Therefore, you can feel free to jump right to the chapters that interest you the most without having to read the earlier chapters first. (Unlike college and law school classes, these chapters don't have any prerequisites.)

Finally, if you're still wondering about the answers to the questions from the previous page, here is a sneak peek:

No, the police definitely do *not* have to read you your rights when they arrest you. In fact, sometimes they can even *interrogate* you without reading you your rights. We'll first explain what *Miranda* rights are, and then we'll show you how the police are able to get around them.

Yes, you *can* be convicted of drunk driving without even driving the car, and even without ever starting up the car's engine. We'll tell you why that is and show you some ridiculous real-life outcomes that have resulted from this incredibly strict law.

Yes, the police can search your home without a warrant. While the warrant is one method for them to get into your home, there are many others. We'll explain several of the exceptions to the warrant requirement and will show you how easily the police can use them to gain access to your home.

Yes, hearsay evidence can be used against you in court. In fact, in a criminal case, it can even be used to convict you of a crime.

How can this be? Well, for starters, there are about *thirty* exceptions to the rule on hearsay. We'll show you exactly how they work.

No, many types of contracts *don't* have to be in writing to be enforceable. We'll tell you about some that do, some that don't, and explain why.

You *might* be able to keep the ring if you break up with your fiancé. Some courts view the ring as a gift, and some courts view it as a conditional gift. We'll explain what all of that means and how it affects whether you can keep the ring.

Finally, after reading this book you might find yourself so interested in the law that you'll want to become a lawyer. In that case, you might be surprised to learn that in some states you don't even have to go to law school to become a lawyer. And in one state, you don't even have to pass the bar exam to become a lawyer.

If you're surprised or intrigued by some of these answers-in-brief, please read on for what we hope is an engaging tour of the lesser-known realities of the law.

Disclaimer—Read This First!

All information in this book is intended only for the purposes of entertainment and enjoyment. This book does not constitute legal advice nor should it be used for legal research or for any other purpose, other than entertainment and enjoyment. No information in this book should be used as a substitute for talking to a licensed attorney who is knowledgeable of the ever-changing laws in the applicable state or states. Reading this book, or even contacting the authors of this book, does not create an attorney-client relationship. Any and all legal questions should be directly posed to a licensed attorney in the applicable state or states. Neither the authors nor the publisher are responsible for any actions taken, or decisions made, by readers of this book.

There are at least four reasons why you should *not* rely on this book for legal advice, or for any other purpose other than entertainment. First, most if not all of the laws discussed in this book will vary from state to state. Even federal laws, including the United States Constitution, will have different interpretations depending on the particular state in which they are applied. For example, what may be *legal* to do in one state may be *illegal* to do in another, and vice versa. As another example, a police action that may violate a citizen's rights in one state, may, in fact, be perfectly acceptable conduct in another. Sometimes this book will discuss the differences between states. Other times, however, it will only discuss the most interesting, and not necessarily the most common, laws and interpretations. And yet other times, it will discuss a "typical" law that is actually a "model" law, or a composite of different states' laws.

Second, many if not most of the laws in our country are heavily dependent on a "facts and circumstances" analysis. This means that the slightest change in a particular person's set of facts and circumstances could lead to a dramatically different outcome under the law. No single book can adequately address all of those subtleties, and this book makes no attempt to do so. Only a licensed attorney in your state will be able to properly assess the subtleties of your particular legal question or issue and give you sound legal advice based on your specific fact situation.

Third, laws are constantly changing. Legislatures, both state and federal, are always drafting new laws and amending old ones. Even the United States Constitution is subject to a constantly changing landscape. For example, the constitutional rights of due process and confrontation are frequently evolving in light of new factual scenarios and new judicial interpretations. What was current at the time this book was written may not be current by the time you read it.

Fourth and finally, this book simply doesn't cover all of the laws that might be relevant to a particular situation. For example, as discussed in chapter 49, you might not be liable for a slander if you speak harmful, but *truthful*, information. But you *might* be liable under different causes of action (that are not even discussed in this book) where "the truth" is *not* a recognized defense. Again, only a licensed attorney in your state will be able to properly advise you based on your facts and the relevant and current law in your state.

Having said all of that, please sit back and enjoy your read as you explore some of the most common myths, oddities, and lies about our legal system.

Acknowledgments

The authors wish to thank the following people, without whom this book would not have been possible:

Our agent, Janet Rosen, Sheree Bykofsky Associates, Inc.
Our editor, Linda Greenspan Regan, executive editor at Prometheus Books

The authors also wish to thank the following people, listed in alphabetical order, for their comments and insight on the legal topics addressed in this book:

Attorney Joseph Easton
Attorney Michael Easton
The Honorable Chad Kerkman
Attorney Sarvan Singh
Assistant District Attorney Brook Teuber
Attorney Robert Teuber
Attorney Scott Wilson

That's a Crime?

Chapter 1
Is it against the law to look at someone the wrong way?

Yes. It certainly can be. And not only might it be against the law, but it might also be considered criminal behavior for which you could wind up with probation, a hefty fine, a jail sentence (which is typically one year or less of incarceration), or, in some cases, even a lengthy prison sentence.

How can this possibly be? Well, it probably begins with our love of government. We love the concept of government so much that we have multiple layers of it. There is the federal government, the state governments, and then the multiple levels of local governments. On top of them, we have a slew of agencies and other governmental bodies, created by each and every level of government, that also have lawmaking authority. These laws consist of statutes, regulations, agency and court decisions, and ordinances, to name only a few. To be sure, we live in a legal maze.

For starters, then, every state government has a massive criminal code that prohibits many types of conduct, such as theft and drunk driving, for example. These criminal codes consist of hundreds, and sometimes a thousand or more, different crimes for which you can be prosecuted and punished. And as if these weren't enough, many of the lower levels of government within each state—such as the counties, cities, villages, and townships—create their own sets of laws called ordinances. Usually, these ordinances replicate the state's criminal code to a large extent, but sometimes they add even more prohibitions on our conduct.

So there may be a local ordinance in effect in your county, city, village, or township. This ordinance prohibits something called "mashing." If you are prosecuted for violating this ordinance, you could be convicted and could face a stiff forfeiture or fine. And if you can't pay, you could eventually receive a "commitment," which is a jail sentence for your failure to pay that fine. What is this ominous-sounding mashing from which our local communities need such vigorous protection? Hang on to your seats; here it is:

> Mashing: no person shall improperly ogle—that is, to eye amorously or provocatively—any person of the opposite sex.[1]

A close reading of this statute raises some interesting issues. First, what is a proper ogle as opposed to an improper ogle? If you properly eye a person amorously or provocatively, it's okay. But if you do so "improperly," it is against this particular law. And how do you know whether it's proper until you do it? Does this mean that only married people can ogle? And if so, how does one get married if he or she can't first ogle?

Second, why are gay men and lesbians excluded from this statute? If you eye someone of the *same* sex in an amorous or provocative manner, you're not violating the ordinance. The most likely explanation is that the government officials who dreamed up this law are somewhat sheltered and never even imagined that two people of the same sex could possibly ogle one another.

This law against mashing is not only on the books, but it actually gets used in prosecution. And the reality can get even worse. There is even a section in most states' criminal codes—the body of law that takes the form of a statute, rather than a noncriminal local ordinance—called disorderly conduct. It is criminal behavior to engage in disorderly conduct, and that crime is punishable with probation, jail time, or, if you have a prior criminal record, possibly even with prison time.[2] Just what is this horrible disorderly conduct that simply has to be criminalized and punished? Here it is:

> Disorderly Conduct: Whoever, in a public or private place, engages in indecent or otherwise disorderly conduct that tends to cause or provoke a disturbance is guilty of a misdemeanor crime.[3]

This disorderly conduct statute has been used, countless times, to convict people for surprisingly minor behavior, including conduct in private places, such as in their own homes. And there is no need to prove that the conduct in question actually caused a disturbance; rather, if such conduct merely "tends to" cause a disturbance, that's enough to qualify as a crime.

So if someone was accused of ogling, an act that upset the person allegedly being ogled, the accused ogler could also be charged with disorderly conduct. How? Well, isn't improper ogling under the mashing ordinance also "indecent" conduct that "tends to cause or provoke a disturbance" under the criminal statute? It sure is. And you might even be convicted of both mashing and disorderly conduct for the same "criminal" act.

This disorderly conduct law is so vague and imprecise that it doesn't give us any notice of what specific conduct is considered criminal. For this reason, its constitutionality has been challenged many times but to no avail. The courts have fallen in love with this disorderly conduct statute, and it is here to stay.

But don't worry. If you don't have a prior criminal record, you might get away with a simple fine rather than jail time or probation, if in fact you are convicted of disorderly conduct.

So, the lesson is that we really need to watch whom we look at or how we appear to look at them these days. Either that, or maybe we should tell our government to stop making so many laws.

Chapter 2
Can you be convicted of drunk driving if you're not driving the car?

Yes. You can be convicted for simply starting up the engine, without ever even driving. In fact, you can even be convicted for simply *turning the key*, even if the engine doesn't start. Perhaps even more surprising, people can be convicted . . . *for driving their wheelchairs.*

First things first. What exactly is drunk driving? Drunk driving, commonly known as OWI (Operating While Intoxicated), DUI (Driving Under the Influence), or DWI (Driving While Intoxicated), seems pretty straightforward. Most of us think of it as being drunk, getting in a car, truck, van, or SUV, and driving down a public road. And if you were to read an actual drunk driving statute, you'd probably think you were right. Consider the wording of this statute:

> Whoever drives or operates a motor vehicle while under the influence of an intoxicant is guilty of the crime of operating while intoxicated.[1]

So far so good, right? Well, you might have noticed some terms that could be open to debate. The most obvious one is the term "under the influence," but let us overlook that one for our purposes. Instead, let us focus on the word "operate." Why do you suppose it is in there? Perhaps the drunk person is not driving the car, but is in the passenger seat, and he's grabbing the wheel or trying to step on the gas. Technically he wouldn't be driving, so it's probably not a bad idea to make it a crime to "operate" a vehicle in addition to "driving" a vehicle. And if you thought that, it certainly would be a logical guess. In fact, the legislature defined the term "operate" as:

The physical manipulation or activation of any of the controls of
a motor vehicle necessary to put it in motion.[2]

That makes sense, doesn't it? If you're a passenger, and someone
else is technically driving, you shouldn't grab the wheel or try to step
on the gas. If you do, it would be (and should be) considered drunk
driving. But, once again, the courts have gotten involved and have
"interpreted" the term "operate" for you. As you might have
guessed, this interpretation leads to some ridiculous outcomes.

Suppose, for example, that you're out one night and you drink
way too much alcohol to drive home. It's winter, it's freezing, and
the bar has just closed. You don't want to call and trouble any of
your friends at this hour, so you decide you'll just get in your safely
and securely parked car, start it up, and crank the heat to keep warm
for a few hours. Then, when morning comes, you'll call a friend for
a ride.

Guess what? You may have just committed the offense of drunk
driving. And if a police officer finds you, you could very well be convicted. Why? Because by turning the motor on, you took a "necessary" step to put the car "in motion." And this isn't just a hypothetical example; people have actually been convicted for this very thing.[3]

But it gets even more interesting. Suppose that it was a warm
night, instead of a cold night, and you just wanted to listen to the
radio while you're falling asleep in your car. So you just turned your
key halfway and never even started the engine. Is *that* drunk driving? It sure can be. Again, how is that? We now know that there's
no requirement that you actually *drive* the car to be guilty of drunk
driving. But don't you have to at least turn it on to be guilty? No.
By simply turning the key halfway to listen to the radio, you've just
"manipulated" or "activated" one of the "controls" necessary to
put the car "in motion." It doesn't matter that you never actually
put the car in motion, or that you never *intended* to do so, or that
you never even started the engine. Nor does it matter that you were
actually acting responsibly, both with regard to the safety of others
and with regard to not waking your friends. Once you turned the
key, that was enough. And again, people have actually been convicted for this and have faced real consequences.[4]

Now you get a sense of how bizarrely courts can interpret things. And if you take a look back at the actual crime of drunk driving, you may notice some other terms with which the prosecutors and the courts could have some fun. What about the term "motor vehicle"? Common sense tells us that the term would include a car, truck, van, SUV, or a similar vehicle that is capable of causing serious harm to other vehicles or people. But what else might a prosecutor try to include in that category? How about a motorized wheelchair?

If you don't think that's possible, just ask the wheelchair-bound Georgia man who got charged with DUI for operating his wheelchair after allegedly drinking vodka.[5] Or ask the Florida woman who suffers from "degenerative disc disease, osteoarthritis and scoliosis," and was busted driving her five-mile-per-hour wheelchair after allegedly having a few too many.[6] And these are just some of the more interesting cases in the area of drunk driving.

At least one judge tried to put a stop to the nonsense, however. The Honorable Peyton Hyslop of Hernando County, Florida, threw out the prosecutor's case against the wheelchair-driving woman on the grounds of fairness and common sense.[7] Of course, Judge Hyslop—a rare bird in today's hypervigilant, tough-on-crime climate—was known as "colorful and controversial" and "too lenient."[8] After throwing out the case, he was replaced as judge by a former prosecutor.[9]

Chapter 3
Can a professional fighter be charged with battery for winning a fight?

Yes. In theory he can be charged. However, whether he could be *convicted* is a different story. To explain further, we first need to understand the various kinds of battery charges, as well the fighter's possible defenses to battery.

First, what constitutes a battery? Battery is a criminal charge that comes in multiple varieties, or degrees, even within a single state. (Battery can also be a "tort," or a civil wrong that is charged in a civil lawsuit between individuals, but our focus will be on *criminal* battery.) For example, a typical misdemeanor battery statute may read something like this:

> Whoever causes bodily harm to another person, without that person's consent, and with the intention of causing them bodily harm, is guilty of misdemeanor battery.[1]

So, if a professional cage fighter manages to break his opponent's nose and knock him unconscious, thereby emerging from the cage match victorious, could he be charged with this particular battery statute? Well, he caused bodily harm to the other fighter, and he intended to do so. But did the other fighter consent to the harm? It's hard to imagine someone consenting to that kind of beating, but isn't that what someone does when he enters the cage or the boxing ring to fight? Certainly, the argument that the losing fighter consented to the beating would be an excellent defense for the winning fighter. But remember, battery charges come in different varieties and degrees, and some of them are felony charges. Here's an example of a typical felony battery charge:

Whoever causes substantial bodily harm—that is, a broken bone or cartilage or unconsciousness—to another person, with the intention of causing any type of bodily harm, is guilty of felony battery.[2]

So, in our hypothetical cage fight, above, could the victorious fighter be charged with this felony battery statute, and if so, how could he defend it? Now, he did cause *substantial* bodily harm, that is, a broken nose and unconsciousness. And he no doubt did so intentionally; after all, that's the goal in a cage fight or boxing match. But didn't we already establish that the other fighter consented? Yes, and consent by the injured person would be a defense to misdemeanor battery, but not to felony battery. If you read the felony battery statute closely, you'll see that the prosecutor does not have to prove a lack of consent by the injured fighter in order to prevail. So, apparently, a person is capable of consenting to *regular* bodily harm—such as a bruise, or pain—but cannot legally consent to *substantial* bodily harm—such as a broken nose or unconsciousness. (The lesson here is that the winning fighter should fight well, but not *too* well.)

So if the losing fighter did not—or more accurately, could not—consent to the beat-down, what defenses might the victorious fighter have? He might be able to claim self-defense. After all, the other fighter was trying to beat him silly as well, so fighting back should be considered self-defense, right? Probably. But self-defense can be justified only if the force used was reasonably necessary to terminate an unlawful attack.[3] And what if the winning fighter, in the heat of battle, happened to break the other fighter's nose *after* he already knocked him unconscious? That certainly wouldn't have been reasonably necessary given that the fighter was already out cold. Or what if the winning fighter struck the first, and only, blow of the fight? *Starting* the fight certainly doesn't count as self-defense, does it?

Does this entire discussion seem a bit absurd? To most people, it certainly would. But the thing about prosecutors is that they have a lot of power—in fact, unchecked and nearly unlimited power—to charge whomever they wish with whatever crimes they wish. Just because a prosecutor can't ultimately *prove* it doesn't mean he can't *charge* it and cause a defendant a ton of grief (not to mention time and money) in the process. Therefore, when prosecutors do these absurd things, defendants may be able to invoke yet another defense—in addition to the consent defense and the claim of self-defense—called the "absurdity doctrine."

The absurdity doctrine can be used as a defense if the plain meaning of a statute—such as the felony battery statute, above—produces an absurd outcome that would be rejected based on common sense. Here's a great example from a different context:

> [I]n *United States v. Kirby*, a sheriff executed an arrest warrant against a mail carrier for murder. A prosecutor then filed charges against the sheriff under a federal statute that made it a crime to willfully interfere with the delivery of the mail. The Supreme Court concluded that the law did not apply in these circumstances, in light of "common sense."[4]

After reading that, you might think that it's not so far-fetched for a prosecutor to charge a professional fighter with battery, especially if the prosecutor wanted to take a stand against violent sports. But if a prosecutor did so, could the victorious fighter use the absurdity doctrine in his defense? He probably could. After all, doesn't common sense dictate that when a state athletic commission formally sanctions a sport, such as boxing or cage fighting, that the participants in the sport not be charged with battery? Certainly, a strong and winning argument could be made. But, the burden and cost of making that argument is on the defendant. A prosecutor loses nothing in charging him in the first place.

Chapter 4
Is marijuana legal?

Yes, but only in some states and only under very specific circumstances.[1]

Across our country, the severity of penalties for smoking marijuana recreationally varies from extremely severe to somewhat lenient. In fact, as a freshman at the University of Michigan in the late 1980s, this author was surprised to see, when crossing the center of campus one April morning, hundreds of students reading, playing Frisbee, and listening to music . . . with nearly all of them smoking pot while doing so!

"What is going on?" this (sheltered) author asked.

"Hash Bash."

"Aren't all these people going to get in really big trouble?" this author persisted.

"Not so much; don't you know about the five-dollar pot law?"

From 1972 to 1990, in the city of Ann Arbor, the possession of less than two ounces of marijuana was a civil infraction that was punishable only by a five-dollar fine.[2] That fine was raised in 1990, but possession of small amounts of marijuana in Ann Arbor still carries no fines larger than a hundred dollars.[3] (This, of course, does not account for the state of Michigan law, or the federal law, both of which criminalize marijuana possession.)

This seemingly lax local law regarding marijuana use is rare, however, and many more communities have instituted extremely strict prosecution and punishment systems for those accused of possessing even the smallest amount of marijuana. An excellent example of this is the state of Wisconsin, where first-time possession is a misdemeanor, and second-time possession, even of an incredibly small amount of marijuana for personal use, is a *felony*.[4] Even more surprising, conviction for this felony crime could result in a multi-year prison sentence.[5] There are also a host of collateral consequences that accompany a felony drug conviction, such as the permanent loss of the right to possess a firearm, the temporary loss of the right to vote, and the loss of many privileges, possibly including access to federal student loans and other federal benefits, depending on the specific crime of conviction.[6] In addition, whether the penalties are stiff or moderate, nowhere in this country is the recreational use of marijuana legal.

What *is* legal, in some states, is the use of medical marijuana where certain severely ill patients—patients who have either a prescription, or in some states a recommendation, from their physicians—are legally allowed to smoke marijuana.[7] In some cases, these patients may even be allowed to grow, for their own consumption, limited amounts of marijuana.[8]

In November of 2008, Michigan became the most recent state to allow "severely ill patients" to "to buy, grow and use small amounts of marijuana" if they are registered with the state.[9] Not all of the states allowing medical marijuana use have developed a state-run registry, but where there is such a registry, the patient must be approved and registered for his or her use of medicinal marijuana to be legal. In all such states, the law clearly limits the amount of marijuana each patient may possess.

In these so-called medical marijuana states, the law governing the medicinal use of marijuana specifically removes state criminal penalties; however, it does not and cannot make reference to federal-level penalties. Under federal law, marijuana is still an *illegal* substance.[10] Opinions differ on whether a person obeying the exact specifications of their state law—for example, an approved and registered patient smoking the prescribed amount of marijuana—should be held in violation of the federal law. Not surprisingly, organizations such as the US Drug Enforcement Administration and the American Civil Liberties Union are on opposite sides of the debate. As of today, however, a hypothetical patient could be prosecuted under federal law for his or her state-sanctioned use of marijuana.[11]

Chapter 5
Can you be convicted of bail jumping if you never leave the state?

Yes. There are many different ways you can find yourself charged with bail jumping. And, perhaps surprisingly, leaving the state *usually* isn't one of them (as long as you make it back for court).

First, here are the basics of how it works: when a prosecutor charges a defendant with a crime, he will usually bring the defendant into court by either having him arrested or, for less serious allegations, issuing a summons and complaint that orders him to appear in court. Then, at the defendant's first appearance in court, a commissioner or judge will set the defendant's bond. Bond is like a contract of sorts between the court and the defendant.[1] Essentially, the court agrees to release the defendant from jail, or allow him to remain out of jail, while his criminal case is pending. In return, the defendant agrees to abide by certain bond conditions imposed by the court.

There are two components of bond: monetary conditions, commonly referred to as bail, and nonmonetary conditions.[2] First, with regard to monetary conditions, the court, depending on the particular defendant and the nature of the allegations, may require that the defendant post some cash bail before being released. In other cases, however, the court may simply allow the defendant to sign his own bond, without posting any cash, which is commonly known as a signature bond or a personal recognizance bond.

Regardless of whether the court imposes a cash bail, however, the court will always impose *non*monetary conditions of bond. These nonmonetary conditions of bond will include, most obviously, the condition that the defendant must appear for all future court dates in the criminal case. Without that bond condition, the defendant would be free to leave and never come back again, without consequence. With that bond condition, however, if the defendant fails to appear for court dates he can be charged with an additional crime, known as bail jumping, for violating bond.[3]

The term "bail jumping" is somewhat of a misnomer, for two reasons. First, when bail jumping occurs, it is a *non*monetary condition of bond, not the monetary condition (bail), that is being violated. Second, bail jumping doesn't require that a defendant "jump," or flee the jurisdiction, at all. In fact, the defendant can be charged with bail jumping for violating *any* of the nonmonetary conditions that a court may choose to impose. What are these nonmonetary conditions? It depends on the nature of the allegations, who made the allegations, and, quite literally, the disposition of the judge or commissioner on that particular day.

Consider the example of a defendant charged with criminal disorderly conduct for arguing with, and yelling and swearing at, his or her spouse. In that case, there is an excellent chance that the court will order the defendant to have "no contact" with the spouse, even if they live together and have children together. And the defendant may be quite surprised when he finds himself charged with a new criminal case for bail jumping just for calling the spouse's residence (formerly the defendant's residence) to talk on the phone in a normal, nonthreatening manner. Although the court never explained it, the term "no contact" doesn't refer to just "in person" contact, which is what allegedly gave rise to the criminal disorderly conduct in the first place. Instead, it likely will be interpreted by the court to mean no contact by phone, e-mail, or text message as well, even though none of that was ever explained.[4]

In addition, if the defendant was alleged to have been drinking during the domestic incident, the court may order him or her not to consume any alcohol during the time the case is pending. The court may even order the defendant to submit to, and pay for, weekly urine testing to ensure that the "no-drink" condition is being followed. Moreover, the yelling, swearing, and arguing with a spouse is enough for the defendant's charge to be considered "violent."

(There is no requirement that an injury even be alleged for the court to consider the allegations violent.) Because the alleged crime is then deemed violent in nature—though both spouses agree that no physical violence took place—the court may order that the defendant not possess any weapons, including hunting weapons, while the case is pending. (A firearm prohibition upon *conviction* of certain crimes can be permanent.)

The possible range of bond conditions that can be imposed by a court is nearly limitless and includes curfews, restrictions on travel, mandated alcohol or other counseling, and periodic check-ins with the court or some other governmental body. In fact, virtually any type of bond condition can be imposed, provided the commissioner or judge on that specific day deems it in the best interest of the state.[5] And if any of these conditions of bond are alleged to be violated—for example, if the defendant were to call his or her spouse on the phone in violation of the no contact order—the state may, and probably will, file bail jumping charges.

And here is what's really surprising to most people: you can be guilty of bail jumping, even if you're completely innocent of the underlying charge that got you placed on bond in the first place. Consider, again, a domestic example. You're accused of and charged with a domestic violence–related crime such as battery, even if you and your spouse agree that no actual violence occurred. You are then placed on bond and ordered to have no contact with your spouse. You think this means no physical contact, so you call your spouse on the phone. Your spouse reports your call to the police, and you're charged with a second criminal case, this one for bail jumping. Even if you were to win your trial on the original case, it doesn't nullify your bail jumping case. Why not? Because the law says that you can still be convicted of bail jumping if, at the time you called your spouse on the phone, you were *accused* of a crime (battery), you were released from custody on bond, and you violated that bond by making the phone call.[6] Whether you actually *committed* the underlying crime of battery doesn't matter one whit.

So, while you might expect an apology from the state and reimbursement of your attorney's fees, what you'll be facing instead is a possible criminal conviction for bail jumping.

Chapter 6
Can you be convicted of a crime for yelling in your own home?

Yes, absolutely. And not only is it possible, but it is also not uncommon. The reality is that the government's reach has now expanded to allow it to control and punish even our nonviolent conduct within our own homes. Of course, we are not talking about loud verbal threats or violent activity; in those cases, the police should be called to intervene. Rather, we are discussing the common, loud family argument.

For such a family argument, a person can be charged with "disorderly conduct" and other similarly named crimes.[1] Disorderly conduct is typically a state-level crime and is prosecuted and punished in state criminal courts throughout our country. In addition to being a crime, it may also be prohibited by a municipal or local ordinance within the same jurisdiction.

But what exactly is disorderly conduct? First, and most alarmingly, it is defined as behavior that occurs "in a public *or private* place."[2] That's right, there is often no requirement that the behavior occur in public. In fact, disorderly conduct can, and often does, consist of behavior such as yelling that occurs right in our homes, where we would typically expect to have the most privacy and freedom.

Second, a person can be guilty of disorderly conduct even if he or she doesn't do anything violent. In fact, in addition to "violence," a person can be convicted of disorderly conduct for engaging in "abusive, indecent, *profane, boisterous* [or] *unreasonably loud*" conduct.[3] Obviously, that's a pretty broad range of behavior and includes many types of conduct, including nonviolent family arguments. And, if the government wants to prosecute you for such an argument but can't quite squeeze your alleged behavior into one of the aforementioned categories, it has created a catch-all category of "otherwise disorderly conduct," which can include virtually any and all types of conduct.[4]

Third, a person's behavior doesn't even have to cause or provoke a disturbance in order for that person to be convicted. Instead, as long as the behavior is the type that "*tends* to cause or provoke a disturbance," then the person can be convicted of disorderly conduct.[5] In fact, the behavior commonly prosecuted under these disorderly conduct-type statutes includes loud arguments between spouses or domestic partners in the home. Once the police are alerted to the situation—for example, by means of a phone call from one of the participants or from a neighbor—the wheels are set in motion for a disorderly conduct prosecution despite the fact that no violence has taken place.

Before we get into the merits of this criminal statute, however, it might be important to ask: what's the big deal? The big deal is that, even though it is just a misdemeanor, disorderly conduct is still a crime. And if convicted of it, you would have a criminal record, which is usually permanent. Even more significantly, if convicted of disorderly conduct in a domestic setting—for example, with a roommate or former roommate, a spouse or former spouse, a person with whom you have a child in common, and possibly even a person you are dating—you may never be able to possess a firearm again.[6] In other words, the constitutional right to bear arms may be lost forever because you engaged in nonviolent conduct—that is, you were loud—within your own home, which caused a disturbance.

Additionally, if convicted of disorderly conduct you may receive a mere fine as a sentence, but you may also receive a jail or even a prison sentence. How? Even though disorderly conduct is typically a misdemeanor, it can be punishable by several months of incarceration. Moreover, these penalties can sometimes be enhanced. If, for example, you had a prior criminal record of some kind, you may be facing two or more years in prison.[7] So, in short, being convicted of disorderly conduct is a *huge* deal.

But this disorderly conduct charge is probably something that is just "on the books" but never really prosecuted, right? What police officer or prosecutor would have time for this is petty, usually non-violent offense? In many cases, the police have no choice but to make the time. In fact, not only has the government expanded its power to be able to reach into our personal lives, but many state governments have also made arrests under this law *mandatory* when the incident occurs within the home.[8] Therefore, even if the police simply want to calm down an argument and then leave, often they can't. Instead, they must make an arrest and set the wheels of the criminal justice system into motion.

Further, the statistics often bear this out: in many counties and states, disorderly conduct is the single most common crime. For example, the state of Wisconsin chooses to treat seventeen-year-olds as adults for criminal law purposes, which brings them into the criminal system while they are still minors. This gives the state the power to start building a criminal record early on in a citizen's life. In fact, in Wisconsin in 2004, less than 2 percent of arrests of seventeen-year-olds were for violent crimes as defined by the Bureau of Justice Statistics.[9] What was the most popular crime for which they were arrested? You guessed it: disorderly conduct. In fact, the runner-up crime, simple possession of marijuana, wasn't even a close second.[10]

To recap, then, we now know that there is an incredibly broad range of behavior that is swept into the criminal statute prohibiting disorderly conduct. In fact, most commonly it includes things as simple as a family argument. We also know how severe the penalties can be for disorderly conduct, including jail time, prison time, and the permanent loss of the constitutional right to bear arms. Finally, we also know that arrests under this statute may be mandatory when the disorderly conduct occurs within the home—the very place where we should have the most freedom to engage in any behavior we want, provided it is nonthreatening and nonviolent.

So, in light of all of this, why do we allow the government such broad reach into our lives to prosecute and convict us of nonviolent crimes within our own homes? Actually, defendants have challenged the disorderly conduct statute numerous times on constitutional grounds. Most commonly, their attorneys argue that the statute is overly broad, criminalizes noncriminal behavior, and doesn't give citizens proper notice of what is, and what is not, criminal behavior. Unfortunately, despite whatever argument is used, it typically fails.

The only way to change this statute appears to be through our state legislatures; that is, the legislatures that inked the law to begin with. However, this is unlikely to happen. In fact, the legislators were able to pass the law in the first place because we citizens allowed them to do so. Unlike the time period of our government's founding, citizens as a whole don't have a healthy distrust *of* government, demand no accountability *from* government, and have little or no participation *in* government. Additionally, with the incomprehensible volumes of laws on the books today, most citizens simply do not even know or care about the disorderly conduct statute, and many other statutes, until they are personally steamrolled by it. Only then will many of us realize the tremendously long and invasive reach of the government into our private lives.

Chapter 7
Can you be convicted of "carrying a concealed weapon" if your gun is *not* concealed?

Yes. And there are other crimes for which you could be convicted as well. In fact, gun-carrying laws often interact with many other laws, including the constitutional right to bear arms, making this one of the most interesting and, in some ways, bizarre areas of criminal law.

Although state laws on this subject can vary greatly, consider the following, which has been slightly simplified from an actual criminal statute:

> A defendant is guilty of the crime of carrying a concealed weapon if: (1) the defendant went armed with a dangerous weapon; and (2) the weapon was concealed. Further, the term "dangerous weapon" includes a firearm, whether loaded or unloaded.[1]

At first glance that may seem straightforward enough. However, even putting aside the federal and state constitutional issues—that is, the constitutional right to bear arms—some problems start to surface when attempting to actually apply this law. For example, let's suppose you're a hunter and want to go to a nearby hunting area to pheasant hunt with your pals. Or, if the idea of shooting birds doesn't appeal to you, suppose you're in a gun club and simply want to go to the range for some target practice. Assuming you have to drive to your hunting area or shooting range, how would you transport your gun? After all, our criminal statute prohibits going somewhere with a concealed gun, doesn't it? Further, unloading it doesn't do any good, as the definition of a dangerous weapon still includes *unloaded* firearms. So what is the answer?

You're no doubt thinking that there's a simple fix to this dilemma. All you would have to do is *not* conceal the gun, right? Simply unload it, put it next to you on the front seat, out in the open in plain view, and drive to the hunting area or shooting range. Then you'd be all right, right? Although that would be good, logical thinking, unfortunately you'd be wrong. As it turns out, the same state that adopted the above law on carrying a concealed weapon also has a specific gun transport law. It states that "no person shall possess or transport a gun in a vehicle *unless* it is encased."[2]

By now, if you're a hunter or a marksman, you're no doubt growing frustrated. If you were to travel with the gun out in the open on the front seat, you're *complying* with the carrying a concealed weapon law, but you're *violating* the gun transport law. However, if you conceal the gun in a case—which seems like the safer and more reasonable thing to do—you're *complying* with the gun transport law, but you're *violating* the carrying a concealed weapon law. In other words, there is no way to go hunting or shooting *and* comply with all of the state's laws.[3]

But things can actually get even sillier. Let's completely forget about the gun transport law and get back to basics. Let's focus *only* on the carrying a concealed weapon law from the above. Clearly, that statute prohibits a person from going armed with a gun that is concealed. So, as we just discussed, transporting the gun out in the open, next to you on the front passenger seat, would comply with the law, right? Actually, no, it doesn't. In fact, one defendant in that state learned the hard way when he was criminally prosecuted, and convicted, for doing just that. But how can that be? After all, the gun wasn't concealed; it was out in plain view on the front seat. Well, the court held that it was, in fact, concealed. Why? Because even though it was out in the open on the front seat, the gun was "indiscernible to the ordinary observation of a person outside" of the vehicle.[4]

Does this mean that the only way to transport a gun in a car is to dangle it out of the car window while driving slowly enough so that everyone can see it? It would seem so; but that, in turn, would lead to prosecution for a host of other crimes, including but not limited to pointing a firearm at another person, recklessly endangering safety, and, most certainly, disorderly conduct. And even putting aside these other crimes for a moment, wouldn't the gun still be "indiscernible" to some people—for example, those outside of and on the *other side* of the moving vehicle? No matter how it is transported—or simply carried, for that matter—wouldn't a gun always be concealed with respect to at least some people? In other words, is it ever possible to fully expose the gun to everyone?

None of this seems to make any sense, but at least we know that in order to be convicted of carrying a concealed weapon, you actually have to carry it somewhere, right? Wrong again. Even though the statute says that you are guilty if you "went armed" with a dangerous weapon, some judges have an odd way of ignoring the plain, ordinary meaning of words, and they instead attach the meaning that they want.

One woman found this out the hard way, when she was arrested and prosecuted under the statute for having a firearm—a gun *without* a firing pin that was therefore *not* capable of actually firing—in her purse while on her front porch. She, of course, argued that she was within her rights as she did not go armed; instead, she was simply staying put on her own property. The court, however, said that even though the statute requires a defendant "went armed" before he or she can be convicted, this does not require that the defendant "actually go somewhere." In other words, and in an attempt at greater sophistication, the court held that "carrying a concealed weapon does not necessarily import the idea of locomotion."[5]

In sum, you're damned if you do (encase the gun) and damned if you don't (encase the gun). So either consult a lawyer in your state about your state's specific laws and how to best comply with them, or give up hunting and shooting and take up checkers instead.

Sex Crimes

Chapter 8
Can you be convicted of "statutory rape" if the minor lied about his or her age?

Yes. As many criminal defendants have learned firsthand, even willful deceit and misrepresentation by the minor about his or her age may not be a viable defense to a statutory rape allegation.

Most people have heard some version of the classic statutory rape scenario. Seventeen-year-old Johnny, for example, has sexual contact with fifteen-year-old Jenny, and is found out. He's arrested and charged with felony sexual assault of a child, more commonly known as statutory rape.[1] Statutory rape, of course, is so named because it really isn't rape; rather, it's only considered against the law because of Jenny's age.

You may have noticed, however, that seventeen-year-old Johnny is also a minor. For our purposes, let's suppose that Johnny lives in a state where a seventeen-year-old minor is considered an adult for criminal law purposes. This makes him the adult, and Jenny the child, even though they're only two years apart in age. In fact, they could even be closer in age than that. Johnny could have just turned seventeen, and Jenny could be turning sixteen tomorrow. But the law sometimes draws hard and fast lines in sex cases, and none of this will matter. Rather, what matters for criminal law purposes is that Johnny is an adult, and Jenny is a child.

The idea behind the statutory rape law is that a person of Jenny's age simply isn't capable of consenting to sexual intercourse, or even sexual contact such as mere touching. We all know that many fifteen-, sixteen-, and seventeen-year-olds willingly have sexual contact, and even sexual intercourse, with their boyfriends and girlfriends who are a year or two older. But the law says they shouldn't be doing this, and if the boyfriend or girlfriend is an adult, then the adult could be convicted of a felony or misdemeanor, often depending on the actual age of the minor.

Most people also know that, once charged with this crime, simply saying that you didn't know the minor's true age may not be a valid legal defense.[2] And there is some logic behind that aspect of the law. If you accept the initial proposition that minors need protection, and therefore any adult who has sex with a minor is a criminal, then it makes sense that the adult shouldn't be allowed to later say that he or she "didn't know" the minor's true age.

But what if the child lied to the adult about his or her age? And not only *that*, but what if the lie was actually believable? And not only *that*, but what if the adult actually made the effort to verify the child's age? What if, after all of that, the "adult" was duped by the "child"? Is that a defense for the adult when he or she is charged with a crime?

The answer, as is often the case, is that it depends on the given state's law. Many states will allow the adult to defend the allegation on this basis and introduce evidence that he or she was duped, or otherwise reasonably believed that the child was an adult. However, some states do not. Some states remain firm and hold the adult "strictly liable" for the crime.

Here's a great example: in one case, a defendant had sex with a minor and was charged with statutory rape. The minor, however, not only told the defendant that she was nineteen, but also told others she was nineteen, appeared to be nineteen, and also had a state-issued identification card showing that she was, in fact, nineteen. But, as it turns out, the identification card was a good fake, and the child was actually only fifteen. The defendant was charged with felony sexual assault of a child and tried to defend himself on the basis that the child fraudulently misrepresented her age, and therefore, he should not be convicted. The court, however, said that the defendant was *not* allowed to introduce *any* of that evidence at trial; rather, if it were proved that he had sexual contact, then he was guilty and was not allowed to put on any defense![3]

Why would any court do this? And why would any prosecutor

want to convict someone of a sex crime under these circumstances? There's no answering the second question, but as to the first question, the court said that such laws—laws known as strict liability statutory rape laws—are necessary to protect children. More specifically, the state has a "strong interest in the ethical and moral development of its children, and this state has a long tradition of honoring its obligation to protect its children from predators and from themselves."[4]

However, the real question is *how* does the conviction in the above example protect the child from predators or from herself? Further, *how* does the conviction teach the child to be moral and ethical? It's tough to imagine. If anything, the child's devious and fraudulent behavior is ignored, as there are simply no repercussions for the child or her actions. And there also seems to be little chance that this conviction would serve as a deterrent to other potential predators. For example, this defendant, now a convicted sex predator, had reason to believe the minor was nineteen, and even took steps to verify her age. It seems unlikely that a person in this position could have done anything more to ensure that the would-be sex partner was not a minor.

And with a conviction for a sex crime such as this one—which was a felony due to the child's actual age—comes all sorts of nasty things, including prison time or jail time, parole or probation supervision, sex offender treatment, sex offender reporting, restrictions on place of residence, the loss of voting rights, the loss of the right to possess a firearm, and difficulty gaining any type of employment, to name only a few of the possible repercussions.[5]

This seemingly unfair and incredibly harsh outcome is one reason why some states *do* allow a defendant to actually put on a meaningful defense against statutory rape charges. In addition, many legal scholars have long called for substantial reform in this area of law.[6]

Chapter 9
Is oral sex illegal?

Yes. In some states, it is illegal.

First, this chapter does *not* address the legality of oral sex as it relates to *non*consensual sex acts. Of course, oral sex is and should be illegal if one of the parties to the sex act does not consent.[1] Additionally, oral sex is and should be illegal if it involves contact between a minor and an adult, which is commonly known as "statutory rape" and carries a wide range of possible penalties, depending, in part, on the age of the minor.[2]

Rather, the question for this chapter is whether oral sex between two clearly consenting adults is illegal in any of our states. The short answer is: yes, in some states, it *is* illegal to have oral sex, even between two consenting adults, and even if those two consenting adults are married to each other. (Whether such prohibitions are still constitutionally valid is another issue altogether.) However, other states' prohibitions on oral sex—long thought by many to be either a throwback to our country's more puritanical days, or a covert way to punish consensual sex acts between homosexuals—have long been repealed.

Nonetheless, oral sex between two consenting adults is either illegal or, until fairly recently has been considered illegal, under the laws of numerous states. The fact that consensual oral sex—viewed as a common practice by many adults—is still considered illegal may seem bizarre. But is there really any harm in having these sex laws on the books if no one is ever arrested and prosecuted for these "crimes"? Unfortunately, there have been people charged, prosecuted, and sometimes even convicted under these laws.

In Virginia, for example, an adult couple found themselves each charged with a "crime against nature"—a felony criminal charge that prohibited oral sex, even in private and even between consenting adults—after a police officer found them engaging in consensual oral sex in a parked car.[3] While both parties are reported to have pled to lesser charges of indecent exposure—a criminal charge that prohibited the public nature of the act, rather than the act itself—the female defendant initially considered challenging the case on constitutional grounds.[4] This challenge would have involved an argument that the state's statute prohibiting oral sex between consenting adults violates our constitutional right to privacy under the United States Supreme Court decision *Lawrence v. Texas*.[5]

In *Lawrence v. Texas*, police officers entered the private residence of an adult male and caught him engaging in sexual conduct with another adult male. The two men were convicted under a Texas statute that prohibited sexual conduct, including oral sex, between homosexuals. The men challenged the statute on constitutional grounds, and when the case eventually reached the United States Supreme Court, the Court ruled that the Texas statute was, in fact, unconstitutional and therefore illegal. The Court stated:

> The present case does *not* involve minors. It does *not* involve persons who might be injured or coerced or who are situated in relationships where consent might not easily be refused. It does *not* involve public conduct or prostitution. It does *not* involve whether the government must give formal recognition to any relationship that homosexual persons seek to enter. The case *does* involve two adults who, with full and mutual consent from each other, engaged in sexual practices common to a homosexual lifestyle. *The petitioners are entitled to respect for their private lives. The State cannot demean their existence or control their destiny by making their private sexual conduct a crime.* Their right to liberty under the Due Process Clause gives them the full right to engage in their

conduct without intervention of the government. It is a promise of
the Constitution that there is a realm of personal liberty which the
government may not enter. The Texas statute furthers no legitimate
state interest which can justify its intrusion into the personal and
private life of the individual.[6]

This is a crucial decision with wide-ranging consequences for the
protection of individual privacy. However, the exact scope and reach
of any United States Supreme Court decision is always open to
debate. For example, the legal "holding" of this case was specifically
limited to the Texas statute and the facts before the court at that
time. Subtle differences in the wording of a statute—such as the class
of persons covered and the exact type of behavior that is prohibited—or subtle differences in the facts of any given case—such as
whether the defendants' conduct was in private or in a semi-public
area—could play a big part in whether any given state law is, in fact,
unconstitutional.

Furthermore, just because this decision was made by the United
States Supreme Court, laws prohibiting oral sex didn't simply dis-
appear. Until they are repealed, or until they are specifically challenged for their unconstitutionality, many laws will remain on the
books and, at least technically, will remain in effect. However,
whether these laws are enforced, and whether they are enforced
evenhandedly, are separate issues altogether.

Chapter 10
Is it a crime to cheat on your spouse?

Yes, in many states adultery is still illegal.

A quick survey of your friends and coworkers might reveal that many of us share the same belief about adultery: that although it is possibly immoral, it certainly is not illegal. Morality issues aside, however, many states still have anti-adultery laws on the books.

Anti-adultery laws vary greatly from state to state. First, the laws vary with regard to definition, with some states characterizing adultery as sexual relations outside of a marriage, while others identify adultery as cohabitating with an individual other than one's spouse.[1] Yet others are even more creative, defining adultery as being lewd and lascivious with someone other than one's spouse.[2]

Second, the laws also vary in severity, with many states classifying adultery as a misdemeanor, while in a few states—like Idaho, Massachusetts, Michigan, Oklahoma, and Wisconsin—it is actually a felony.[3] Third, the laws also vary regarding who can be convicted and punished under the law. Most states have the ability to prosecute both parties in the affair, while a minority of states may prosecute only the married party.[4] In other states, the law is more complex and focuses not only on the marital status, but also the sex—that is, male or female—of the parties.[5]

By way of example, one penal code, in which adultery is defined as "the sexual intercourse of 2 persons, either of whom is married to a third person,"[6] allows for a penalty of as much as four years in prison.[7] While another penal code defines adultery in a similar fashion—as one who "engages in sexual intercourse with another person at a time when he has a living spouse, or the other person has a living spouse"[8]—the crime is classified as a misdemeanor, for which the maximum penalty is a mere five-hundred-dollar fine or ninety days in jail.[9]

How did we end up with these anti-adultery laws in the first place? In the oldest of our United States, they are a result of British common law that sought to punish numerous sexual acts, including oral sex and sex between unmarried people.[10] In other states, anti-adultery laws were added to the books as a result of the anti-vice movements of the 1920s and 1930s.[11] Previously, adultery often related to matters of civil law, specifically civil torts that were known as "heart balm actions" and were intended to prevent the broken heart of a spouse.[12] "Heart balm actions," which included prohibitions against enticing another man's wife to abandon him and appropriating the affections of a married individual away from his spouse, have largely been abolished.[13]

Furthermore, although contemporary courts have at times played host to criminal charges under the anti-adultery laws, these instances have certainly decreased in modern times. One possible reason for this, of course, is that some "of the officials responsible for the enforcement of this law are currently or have previously engaged in adulterous activities themselves."[14] So why, then, do these seemingly outdated laws continue to exist in so many states? In other words, under what legal circumstances are these laws still relevant?

First, anti-adultery laws are still relevant in that people can, even in our modern times, be prosecuted under them. Second, although an unintentional result of their development, anti-adultery laws can figure largely into divorce proceedings. Before states instituted no-fault divorce proceedings, adultery was one of the most popular grounds for divorce, and to this day it may be listed as the grounds for divorce in states that retain the fault-divorce option.[15]

There are additional applications of anti-adultery laws in divorce; one in particular may be surprising:

> Since adultery is a crime, an adulterous spouse can refuse to testify in the course of a divorce case, invoking the Fifth Amendment

right against self-incrimination. In other words, precisely because adultery is a crime, the adulterous spouse can avoid admitting his or her transgression, even in civil proceedings.[16]

Consequently, the result of invoking the Fifth Amendment during divorce proceedings may actually serve to benefit the philandering spouse, since he or she now has legal protection against answering questions about his or her unfaithful exploits.

Proven adulterous behavior may also play a role in the property distribution during a divorce. A judge's decisions regarding post-divorce division of property, and even the awarding of alimony, may favor a wronged spouse in those states where the judge is to factor marital fault into his or her decision.[17]

However, there is at least one place where adultery is still a big deal. One government institution that seems to take adultery seriously is our military. In fact, members of the military are far more likely than civilians to be prosecuted for adulterous behavior. However, those charged with adultery in the military are being charged with breaking the military criminal code, which "bars married servicemen from having extramarital sex and unmarried servicemen from sleeping with married people," rather than being charged under the anti-adultery laws of one of our states.[18] This subjects them to a range of military, instead of state, sanctions.

Chapter 11
Is prostitution legal in Las Vegas?

No. Prostitution is not legal in Las Vegas.

Many tourists to the "sin city" make the trip under the false impression that prostitution is legal in Las Vegas. It's an understandable mistake, given the city's reputation as an epicenter of vice. That Las Vegas's own tourism agency has promoted the city with the phrase "What happens in Vegas, stays in Vegas" does little to diminish the idea that Vegas is a vacation destination where inhibition is thrown by the wayside.

Interestingly, Nevada state law prohibits legalized prostitution in counties with more than 400,000 people, which includes Clark County, in which Las Vegas is located.[1] The state, however, does allow smaller counties to decide for themselves whether to allow legalized prostitution, and several smaller Nevada counties do indeed allow it. The closest county to Las Vegas hosting legalized prostitution is Nye County, more than sixty miles east of the city.[2]

Over the years, various attempts have been made to change state law in order to allow prostitution in Las Vegas. The most recent attempt was defeated in early 2009. Some interested parties had been in the process of drafting a bill that would have established a limited number of state-licensed brothels as a pilot program. In exchange, the brothel industry, which is not currently taxed by the state, offered to pay state taxes.[3] However, before the bill was even completed, the Nevada state legislature informed the parties involved that it would not be considering the proposal.[4]

If one wants to experience legal prostitution while in Nevada, one can visit any number of brothels, called "ranches," in one of the state's other counties. These brothels are licensed and regulated by the state, which includes regular health checks for the workers.[5] In early 2009, a woman who decided to auction off her virginity online seems to have escaped prosecution by arranging for the transaction to take place in Nevada's Moonlite Bunny Ranch. Of course, some people questioned whether the woman was breaking federal law by advertising on the Internet. However, those officials who were interviewed declined legal action, since the transaction was being advertised from, and was set to take place in, one of Nevada's licensed brothels.[6]

However, Las Vegas's designation as "sin city" is not necessarily a misnomer. Besides legalized gambling, the city offers lawful erotic diversions such as strip clubs, fetish clubs, "swingers" clubs, and escort services.[7] Of course, one should not assume that prostitutes fail to ply their trade within Las Vegas city limits. There is prostitution in the "sin city," but those who offer it and those who accept it are participating in an illegal act. In addition to the threat of prosecution for the act itself, Las Vegas prostitutes and their customers also open themselves up to abuse, fraud, robbery, or other mistreatment.

Interestingly, in our country's early days, prostitution was highly regulated and *not* illegal. During the turn of the century, the country began instituting a number of "progressive" changes, such as drug regulation, pure food requirements, and antitrust laws.[8] One part of this movement was antiprostitution interest groups, who felt that prostitution was both a threat to family unity and the principal means by which venereal disease was spread.[9] By the end of World War I, prostitution was made illegal in most states. It continues to be prohibited nearly a century later, due to concerns that legalizing the trade would lead to increased violence, promote the mistreatment of women, and contribute to human sex slave trafficking.[10]

However, some researchers contend that legalizing prostitution may not necessarily have such negative results. Some look to Sweden as a prototype that might be emulated elsewhere in the world. Sweden has made it legal to offer prostitution services, but not to purchase such services. In other words, it is solely the clients, and not the workers, who face criminal charges.[11] Some laud this model as one that is both legally "reasonable" to the workers, yet legitimately discourages potential clients. In fact, as Sweden's arrest rate of prostitutes' clients has risen, the number of prostitutes has significantly decreased.[12] Others feel the example set by Sweden is ineffective and even dangerous, in that it may be enticing a more aggressive clientele to the country.[13]

Regardless of one's views, it would be unrealistic to expect prostitution to be legalized in a widespread way in the United States any time soon. Instead, lawmakers and special interest groups across the country are likely to continue to uphold and enforce the current laws prohibiting prostitution. In fact, except for select counties in Nevada, prostitution is illegal across the United States, with one little-known exception: Rhode Island.

In the state of Rhode Island, there is a so-called prostitution loophole. While it is expressly illegal to engage in street prostitution or to operate a brothel, there is no law on the books in that state prohibiting acts of prostitution that take place in a private residence.[14] Although a persistent issue within the Rhode Island state legislature, as of early 2009, individuals in that state can sell and buy acts of prostitution and remain exempt from prosecution as long as the act itself takes place inside an individual's home. Given the narrow scope of this loophole, however, it seems unlikely that Rhode Island will be passing Nevada in tourism volume anytime soon. In fact, later in 2009, after this chapter was first written, the Rhode Island legislature closed its indoor prostitution loophole.[15]

Problems with the Police

Chapter 12
Do the police have to read you your rights when they arrest you?

No. This is perhaps the most common myth in criminal law.

First, why do so many of us believe this myth? Probably because we've seen it played out countless times in movies and television dramas. The cop, after cracking the case, arrests the bad guy and reads him his rights: "You have the right to remain silent, and anything you say could be used against you in a court of law!" In movies and television, the police do this routinely, almost like a victory speech at the end of every episode. In reality, however, the police rarely do this; nor are they required to under the law.

The "rights" to which the above question refers are *Miranda* rights, or *Miranda* warnings, so named after the United States Supreme Court case *Miranda v. Arizona.* To begin with, what exactly is a *Miranda* warning? When the police give you a *Miranda* warning, they must inform you that: (1) you have the right to remain silent; (2) you have the right to an attorney, and if you cannot afford an attorney, one will be appointed for you; and (3) anything you say may be used as evidence against you.[1] There is no precise language that must be used; rather, it is the substance of what is said that counts. Some police officers may tell you that you have additional rights as well; for example, if you choose to answer questions, you can change your mind and stop talking at any time.

The fact is, however, that the police do *not* have to give you the *Miranda* warning when they arrest you. Under the law, the police only have to give you the warning if you are *both* under arrest *and* they intend to interrogate (question) you.[2] This is a crucial point, and one that the police will use to their advantage. For example, in many police investigations, when the police first arrest a suspect, they are only beginning, rather than ending, their investigation. In order to make a case they'll need all the evidence they can get. Therefore, when the police arrest you, they have no incentive whatsoever to read you your rights. If they were to do that, you might actually choose to exercise your rights and remain silent, which would be bad for them. However, if you don't know your rights, you might start talking and may even blurt out something that would incriminate you and help their case. The police know this, and they certainly won't discourage you from talking by reading you your rights. Instead, they'll simply arrest you, shut their mouths, and see if you start singing like a song-bird. (Which, surprisingly, many arrestees do.)

But the police may also take a different approach. After they arrest you, instead of keeping quiet and going about their business, they may decide to *tell* you things. If they're *telling* you things, rather than *asking* you questions, this doesn't count as interrogation, and they still don't have to read you your rights.[3] And they know that some of the things they *tell* you may get you talking, which is what they want. For example, the police may arrest you and tell you "your neighbor Bob saw you break into his garage last night. That's a pretty serious accusation." If you respond to this accusation, it would be great for the police, but it won't help you one whit: you're already under arrest and you're not going any-where, except to the police station.

Suppose, for example, that you respond to this accusation by saying: "I just went to his garage to borrow his rake. It's never been a problem before!" However, what you just did is admit to being on Bob's property, which is a necessary component of the crime with which they want to charge you. And because their "statement" to you (about what Bob allegedly said) was not in the form of a "ques-tion," they technically didn't interrogate you. Therefore, they were not required to read you your rights, and they easily got an incrim-inating statement from you.

But there is another technique that police can use to get around *Miranda* as well. Suppose the police suspect you of a crime, and they really want to question you. But you're a savvy guy or gal, and they know that. It would be too risky a strategy for them to hope that you'll just start talking on your own. Sure, they could arrest you, take you downtown, and *then* start questioning you. But in that case, there would be *both* an arrest *and* an interrogation, and they'd first have to read you your rights. So how do they get around that? They can simply walk up to you, in a public or even a private place, and just start interrogating you. In this case, there is, in fact, an interrogation, but this time you're not technically under arrest. Therefore, once again, they can skip the *Miranda* warning.[4] Besides, there's no real risk for them in this strategy. You probably wouldn't run away when they start questioning you, and if you did, the police would just catch you and arrest you anyway. Therefore, the old "interrogate first and arrest second" strategy is a very common and effective tactic for the police.

On top of all this, what good is the *Miranda* warning anyway? If you're really paying attention to it, you may actually be confused rather than informed. Read the warning again. This may actually raise more questions than it answers. For example, assume that you decided to ask for an attorney. That's "saying" something, isn't it? And anything you "say" can be used against you as evidence, at least according to the warning. So, if you go to trial, wouldn't the prosecutor be able to tell the jury that you refused to talk and instead requested a lawyer, thereby making you look guilty?

Yes, asking for a lawyer *is* saying something. And yes, anything you say *can* be used against you. So it would be logical to think that your request for a lawyer could be used against you at your trial, and this might persuade you *not* to request a lawyer. But if you thought that, you'd probably be hurting your own case. Generally speaking, the law states that your post-*Miranda* request for a lawyer cannot be used against you in court.[5] So the warning really isn't that accurate or informative to begin with.

Conversely, what if you remained silent? Can that *silence* be used against you as evidence? The warning doesn't really address that. And can you both have a lawyer *and* refuse to answer police questions, or is it one or the other? And if you get a lawyer, can anything you say still be used against you as evidence? And if so, what's the point of getting a lawyer before the police interrogate you?

Hmmmm.

So remember, unless there is *both* an arrest *and* an interrogation (questioning), the police *don't* have to read you your rights. Keep in mind, however, that you still *have* those rights; it's just that the police don't have to tell you about them.

Chapter 13
Can the police search your car if you have an air freshener hanging on the mirror?

Yes. At least it can be one of the factors that can justify a police search after a traffic stop.

Most of us know how easy it is to get pulled over when driving our cars. All it takes to justify a police stop is something as simple as speeding, an expired sticker on a license plate, slowing down but not stopping at a stop sign, or even a minor lane deviation. But sometimes the police will want to do more than just stop you and issue a citation. Sometimes, they'll want to detain you and search your car and its contents.

So under what circumstances may the police not only stop your car but also detain you and search your car? The police must first have what's called "probable cause" to believe that your car contains evidence of a crime, or contraband, which often means illegal drugs.[1] This concept of probable cause is as vague of a concept as you'll find in our legal system. The law says that in order to have probable cause, the police officer must have more than a mere hunch that your vehicle contains drugs. However, all he needs is a reasonable belief, under all of the facts and circumstances, that there is a fair probability that drugs or other evidence of a crime will be found in your car.[2] If he thinks that there is probable cause, then the officer may search your vehicle, and there's nothing you can do about it.

So what about the air freshener hanging from your mirror? Is that probable cause? The police could argue that an air freshener is enough, because in their experience, people who have drugs in their cars like to cover up the odor with air fresheners. But, air fresheners could also be used for any number of innocent reasons. Maybe you're trying to mask other odors, such as dog or cat odors. Or maybe you just like the smell of the miniature, alpine-scented tree hanging from your rearview mirror. (Besides, it matches the school colors on your high school graduation tassel and looks pretty good hanging there.) Therefore, the police may need a touch more to get past the point of a "mere hunch" and into the land of "probable cause."

Remember, it all comes down to the so-called facts and circumstances surrounding the traffic stop and the other events that led up to the search. What are some of these facts and circumstances? There are many, and all it takes is one or two of them—with or without the presence of an air freshener, actually—to justify a search of your car. For example, have you ever eaten fast food in your car and not cleaned up the wrappers right away? Some of us probably have a McDonald's wrapper or two sitting in our car right now. That, it turns out, is a fact or circumstance that tends to give rise to probable cause to believe that you've got drugs in your car. But what the heck does a McDonald's wrapper have to do with whether you're carrying drugs in your car? And in fact, wouldn't a messy car with garbage in it tend to *explain* the need for the air freshener? Logically, yes, but not so much in our legal system.

Here's a great quote from a court decision where probable cause was found to exist, and therefore the detention and search of the car was held to be legal and valid. This quote illustrates the integral role of fast-food wrappers in the determination of probable cause: "Trooper Brown suspected that drugs were in the car given a number of factors that in his experience indicated the existence of a drug courier: the heavy odor of air freshener, the cellular phone, Patterson's nervous disposition, and fast-food wrappers strewn around the car."[3]

Yes, that quote is for real. And you might have noticed some other, equally suspect "facts and circumstances" that this court relied on in finding there was probable cause that the car contained drugs. How about the cell phone? It is quite unlikely that a cell phone could be probative of drug trafficking, otherwise every teenager in the country would be considered a drug dealer.[4] And what about the nervous disposition? Is there anyone who is *not* nervous when pulled over by the police?

There are other interesting factors that can be used to justify a vehicle search as well, and some of them are nearly as entertaining as the fast-food wrappers. (They're entertaining unless, of course, you're the one being stopped and searched.) For example, the police can even look at how you were driving your car *before* you were pulled over. If they feel (or say) that you had a "tense posture while driving," this also could be used against you as an indicator that you had drugs in your car.[5]

So far we have seen that tense driving and nervous behavior can justify a police search. And those two things seem to be somewhat negative in nature, and certainly closely related. After all, who likes a tense, nervous driver? So you would think that if you're relaxed and easy-going, you'd be in the clear, right? Not necessarily. One court found probable cause, and therefore upheld a vehicle search, because the driver exhibited "talkative, and overly-friendly behavior."[6] Seemingly, you're damned if you do, and damned if you don't.

Keep in mind that any of these facts or circumstances—combined with a dangling air freshener, or even just the scent of an air freshener emanating from somewhere in the car[7]—can catapult the police down the path and into the land of probable cause, thereby justifying their search. But there are other facts and circumstances that don't even relate to your demeanor or disposition. For example, sometimes just being in a particular state or heading in a certain direction will give rise to probable cause. Let's say you're heading out of California and driving to Las Vegas for the weekend. The fact that you are leaving the state of California—even though you *have* to leave California in order to *get* to Las Vegas—is a factor that supports a finding of probable cause. Why? Because California might be considered a "source state for illegal narcotics."[8]

And you'd better hope you're not on a really long trip. If the police see NoDoz in your car, that too can be a factor leading to probable cause to believe that there are illegal drugs in your car.[9] And you'd best not be out on a casual Sunday drive somewhere, with no real destination in mind. If the police ask you where you're headed and you give them a "vague description of travel plans," that will be another factor leading to the reasonable belief that you are transporting drugs, and therefore will help to justify the search of your car.[10]

In summation, an air freshener, or just the scent of an air freshener, in and of itself, may not be enough to justify a search of your car. However, once that is combined with any personal characteristic (such as nervousness, tenseness, talkativeness, or friendliness), any other physical object (such as a cell phone, fast-food wrappers, or NoDoz), or any travel-related characteristic (such as a meandering drive *in* California, or a drive *out of* California), you could be well on your way to a police search.

Chapter 14
Can the police tell when you are lying?

No. Despite the myth to the contrary, the police are no better than the rest of us, and no better than mere chance, at detecting deception. But if you guessed otherwise, you're certainly not alone.

In a recent survey with a very large and very educated sample size, 88 percent of respondents were either uncertain or *agreed* with the proposition that "compared to the general public, police officers are more skilled at recognizing when a person is lying."[1] Further, 95 percent of respondents were either uncertain or *agreed* that "if an individual is properly trained, he or she can detect lying by observing a person's body language."[2] No doubt playing on these beliefs, the television series *Lie to Me* is centered on a highly trained government agent who can "uncover the deepest secrets and crack the hardest cases."[3] How does he do it? He "read(s) clues embedded in the human face, body, and voice to expose the truth in criminal investigations," of course.[4]

When claims of human lie detecting are put to the test, however, they fall by the wayside along with all other pseudoscientific claims. In fact, a recent controlled, scientific study tested the notion that we can somehow know when people are lying to us. But it went even further and divided the test subjects (the would-be human lie detectors) into two groups: those trained in detecting lies, and those who had no prior training or experience. The study then "tested the hypothesis that training in the use of verbal and nonverbal cues increases the accuracy of these judgments."[5]

The study produced results consistent with prior studies. Specifically, people were "unable to distinguish between truthful and deceptive suspects."[6] What was really interesting, however, was that while those who were trained in the detection of lies "were more confident and cited more reasons for their judgments," they were actually less accurate.[7]

As indicated earlier, the results of this study were consistent with other similar studies that were properly and scientifically designed. For example, another study found that one's ability to detect lies was *not* improved by either "training or prior experience."[8] The study further found that those with training in lie detection were no better than mere chance at actually detecting the liars.[9] Time and again, the notion that police can be human lie detectors is disproved, yet the myth remains.

So what's the harm in this misconception? The harm occurs when a person is falsely accused of a crime and denies any wrongdoing, yet the police believe, based on their training and experience, that the person is, in fact, lying. The harm is that not only may the person get *charged* with a crime, but also, based on the misconception that police are able to detect liars, the person may actually get *convicted* of a crime. Consider this example:

Suppose your spouse accuses you of child abuse. You're innocent, but your spouse is making the accusation in the context of a heated divorce and is highly motivated to do whatever it takes to beat you in the custody battle. (And if you think this type of gamesmanship doesn't happen, just ask a local divorce attorney or criminal defense attorney.) Your spouse reports the alleged abuse to the police, who call you on the phone and ask you to come down to the police station to give your side of the story. You don't bother consulting with a lawyer; you know you're innocent and are convinced that you can clear this up once you talk to the police. At the police station, you're taken to a small room, where the officer interrogates you and, as he is trained to do, asks you some accusatory questions and aggressively tests your version of the events. You admit to having custody of your child on the weekend in question, but you deny any wrongdoing whatsoever. You explain your side of it, as well as your spouse's motivation for making this false accusation. The officer, however, reads your facial expressions and body language, as he is trained to do, and is convinced that you're lying. He also lets you know this by *accusing* you of lying and refusing to accept your explanations.[10]

When the interrogation is over, you are lucky that you are allowed to walk out of the police station. However, much to your surprise, two weeks later you receive a summons and criminal complaint in the mail, commanding you to appear in criminal court for your felony child abuse case. Not only have you been charged, but you later learn that your interrogation was recorded (as is now mandatory in some states), and this video recording is admissible evidence against you, even though you denied the allegation. Now the jury will get to hear and see the police officer rejecting your version of events and accusing you of lying to him.

So what's the harm in all of this? Remember, most people think that police officers can detect who is lying. Worse yet, they've heard this officer specifically accusing *you* of lying. At your trial for felony child abuse, an allegation that you deny, you could well be convicted based not on physical evidence, since there is none, but rather on the misconception that police can act as human lie detectors. This myth about the police and their ability to detect lies, then, can prove to be very harmful to you, as you could get yourself a felony conviction. This means that you could be barred from having any contact with your child, and could even see prison or jail time.

But even if your interrogation was not recorded, the police may still be allowed to testify at your trial that you were lying when you denied guilt. To begin with, there is a general rule that one witness cannot testify that another witness is lying. Why? Because judging the truthfulness of witnesses is a function that must be left to the jury, not to other witnesses.[11] However, the prosecutor and the police have developed many ways around this general rule. For example, if a police officer questioned you at your home, and then came back to question you a second time, the officer's version of what you said at both of those interrogations is admissible against you at your trial, whether or not it was recorded.[12] And if the prosecutor asks the officer, at trial, why he went back to interrogate you a second time, the officer could simply answer that you lied to him the first time, and he went back the second time to get the truth.[13]

How can that possibly be admissible in court, given the rule that one witness is not allowed to testify as to the truthfulness of another witness? In one case, the court held that the testimony was used *not* to prove the defendant was a liar, but rather to explain why the officer went back for the second interrogation.[14] Sure, the officer's decision-making process and investigative tactics were completely irrelevant to whether the defendant committed the crime, but once this alternative explanation is accepted by the court, the jury gets to hear the officer's opinion that the defendant lied. This, combined with the commonly held misconception that police are able to act as human lie detectors, could once again result in conviction based not on evidence, but rather on the pseudoscientific belief about the mental powers of the police.

So the lesson here—other than it's usually a bad idea to talk to police without legal representation, even if you know (or believe) you are innocent—is that potential jurors should be educated that police are no better than average citizens, which is to say no better than mere chance, at detecting a lie.

Chapter 15
Can the police lie to you when they interrogate you?

Yes. The police are allowed to use a variety of tactics when interrogating suspects. Lying—which includes the fabrication of physical evidence and eyewitnesses—is perfectly acceptable for them.

When a suspect is interrogated by police and ultimately gives a statement, the prosecutor may later want to use that statement against the defendant (formerly the suspect) at his criminal trial. Depending on what was actually said, however, the defendant and his lawyer may want to suppress the statement, or keep it out of evidence at trial. One of the arguments that the defendant may use is that the statement was not made freely and voluntarily, but rather was made under the pressure of coercive police interrogation, and therefore its use at trial would violate the defendant's constitutional rights. Therefore, the trial judge, in deciding whether the statement is admissible, will hold a hearing. At the hearing he will consider, among other things, the tactics that the police used in order to obtain the defendant's statement. And, lying and fabricating evidence is perfectly legal.[1] Here's a hypothetical, but typical, example of a two-on-one, good-cop/bad-cop interrogation:

> **Bad Cop:** Look, Johnny, we know you committed this burglary last night at your neighbor's apartment, now just admit it and things will go better for you.
> **Johnny:** No, Officer, I didn't do it. I was home all night; I didn't even leave my apartment. I *did* drink a lot of alcohol last night . . . but I know I wasn't at that apartment.
> **Bad Cop:** Don't give us that! We've got two eyewitnesses that saw you

go into the apartment, and we've got your prints on the door. We know you did it, and we've got the evidence to prove it.

Johnny: No, no! That can't be . . . it couldn't have been me.

Bad Cop: Forget him, I'm going to write up the report and throw the book at him. Good Cop, you sit here with him until I'm done.

Johnny: No, wait, it wasn't me!

Good Cop: Look, Bad Cop gets a little surly sometimes, but he means well. I'll tell you what, maybe you didn't mean to commit this crime, because you were so drunk, and maybe it wasn't even your idea to do it, am I right?

Johnny: Ummmm . . .

Good Cop: Now look, I'm here to help you. Either you meant to break into the apartment and intentionally steal your neighbor's property, or things just worked out that way. I mean, it really wasn't even you, in a way; it was just the alcohol, right? You cooperate with me now and, in my experience, the system will make things much, much easier on you.

Johnny: Well, I didn't mean to do anything . . .

Good Cop: That's right, it wasn't even your idea; someone else probably came up with the idea, and you just went along with it because of the alcohol . . .

Johnny: Yeah, I guess that was it. I mean, if you got my prints on the door and people saw me going in there . . . I suppose it had to be the alcohol . . .

Now, what happened here is that Johnny initially denied the allegation, and the police fabricated evidence against him, specifically, the two eyewitnesses and the fingerprint evidence. (If the police really *had* this evidence, they wouldn't have bothered interrogating Johnny in the first place.) Then, on top of that, they offered Johnny two alternatives from which to choose: (1) you did this crime, you intended to do this crime, and you're going to get the book thrown at you; or (2) you did this crime, but you didn't mean to do it, it wasn't even your idea, it really wasn't even *you* due to the alcohol, and things will go real easy for you if you cooperate. (Notice that "you're *completely* innocent of all wrongdoing" is *not* one of the alternatives.)[2]

Johnny chose the second, and most attractive, of the two alternatives and wound up convicted of felony burglary based on his confession. As it turns out, the fingerprint and eyewitness evidence was fabricated and, much to Johnny's surprise, "the system" was *not* easier on him as a result of his unwittingly confessing to a felony. (The officer's statement that the system would be easier on Johnny was probably not improper, as he was only speaking as to his own personal opinion, and was not making direct promises of leniency, despite the way that Johnny may have *interpreted* the officer's statements.)

So what's the problem? A guilty man confessed to a crime, right? Yes, that could be the case, and often is the case. After all, most of us innocent people would like to think that, if confronted with fabricated evidence by two skilled police officers in an intimidating interrogation room, we would laugh in their faces and call them out as the frauds they are. We would also like to think that, when confronted with two unattractive alternatives under the pressure of skilled police interrogation, we would assert that both alternatives are false and instead further a *third* alternative is actually the truth: that we didn't commit the crime at all.

Despite our own inner confidence, however, not all criminal suspects are that confident or self-assured. Many suspects, like Johnny, are intoxicated at the time of the alleged crime, or even at the time of the interrogation, or are going through alcohol withdrawal. Others are juveniles or are mentally impaired, and are highly suggestible and compliant with authority figures such as police. Others have horrible memories and, in light of fabricated evidence that they *believe* to be true, become convinced that they did, in fact, commit the crime. Yet others are mentally ill and are seeking notoriety and attention. In all of these cases, these types of suspects are very likely to confess to a crime they did not commit.[3] Consequently, not only is an innocent person in grave danger of being convicted, but the guilty person will go free.

The main reason that false confessions lead to convictions is that jurors have an incredibly difficult time imagining that someone would confess to a crime that he or she did not commit. In fact, in a recent study with a large sample size of highly educated respondents, 73 percent believed that an innocent person would either never confess to a crime, or would only confess after strenuous pressure by police.[4] However, the reality is that in today's world of post-conviction DNA exonerations, research has shown that many innocent people have been convicted of serious crimes based largely, if not entirely, on their own false confessions.[5] Further, many of these false confessions were induced by very minimal police pressure, such as the interrogation tactics described in this chapter.

Therefore, while police interrogation tactics, including lying and falsifying evidence, may seem like a good thing because they more easily lead to convictions, one of the serious and immeasurable drawbacks is that many of those convictions are of innocent defendants.

Chapter 16
Can the police search your home without a warrant?

Yes, they can.

First, let's begin with the general rule, which states that police may *not* enter or search a person's home unless they have a warrant. A warrant is a written document, signed by a neutral and detached judge, ordering the police to enter a person's home and search it for a very specific purpose. These warrants should be issued only upon reliable, sworn statements that give the judge good reason to believe that the targeted home contains evidence of a crime. The purpose behind the warrant requirement is explained by the Supreme Court of the United States as follows:

> [T]he physical entry of the home is the *chief evil* against which the wording of the Fourth Amendment is directed. And a principal protection against unnecessary intrusions into private dwellings is the warrant requirement imposed by the Fourth Amendment on agents of the government who seek to enter the home for purposes of search or arrest. It is not surprising, therefore, that the Court has recognized, as a basic principle of Fourth Amendment law, that searches and seizures inside a home without a warrant are *presumptively unreasonable*.[1]

More specifically:

> The point of the Fourth Amendment, which often is not grasped by zealous officers, is *not* that it denies law enforcement the support of the usual inferences which reasonable men draw from evi-

dence. Its protection consists in requiring that those inferences be drawn by a neutral and detached magistrate *instead* of being judged by the officer engaged in the often competitive enterprise of ferreting out crime. . . . The right of officers to thrust themselves into a home is . . . a grave concern, not only to the individual but to a society which chooses to dwell in reasonable security and freedom from surveillance.[2]

Given this stern language condemning warrantless police searches, under what circumstances would the court actually *permit* a warrantless search? You might think the situations would be few and far between, but that's not the case. In fact, there are many exceptions to the warrant requirement, and we will now look at some of the more popular ones.

In order to *search* your home, the police have to first find a way to *enter* your home. There are several ways for police to legally gain access, even without a warrant. The first, not surprisingly, is your consent. If the police ask you if they can enter your home, and you say yes, then you've waived your constitutional right to privacy and the police may enter. However, it doesn't have to be that clear-cut. First, you do not have to waive this right intelligently and knowingly. In other words, unlike your *Miranda* right to remain silent, the police do not have to first explain your right of privacy or make sure that you understand it before they obtain your consent.[3] And second, your consent doesn't even have to be expressly given. If, under the right facts and circumstances, the police simply enter your home and you fail to object or stop them, you may have just given *implied* consent, which will waive your rights just as quickly as expressly saying, "Yes, you can enter."[4]

Consent can also be given by a third party. Suppose you're out of the house one night, and the police want to enter and search your house without a warrant. If someone else is at the home—say, a babysitter—and that person expressly stated or even implied that the police may enter, that consent could very well validate the entry and subsequent search. This would be true even if the person who gave consent didn't have your permission or the authority to do so. As long as the police reasonably believed the person had the authority, even if their belief was mistaken, that could be enough to validate their actions.[5]

Another way police can gain access to your home is by using the hot pursuit doctrine. If the police are chasing a person—whether it's you or even some unknown person—and the person goes into your home, the police may be allowed to follow him into your home to search for him and arrest him. In this case, the police don't even need to *see* the person physically enter your home. As long as they were chasing the person and have reason to believe that he or she *could* have gone into your home, that is reason enough.[6]

Police may also enter your home without a warrant if there is some type of exigent circumstance, or perceived danger to themselves or to others. A classic example is where the police receive a phone call reporting some type of fight or violence. Then, upon arrival, they hear screaming inside of the home. Under these circumstances, police do not have to stop and obtain a warrant; if they waited that long, they would probably be too late to do any good. Rather, they can simply enter the home to respond to the ongoing crime and to protect people inside from further harm. However, the situation need not be this dire in order to justify a warrantless entry. For example, police may even justify the entry into constitutionally protected areas based on a report of underage drinking. Why would a court allow this? Because the report of underage drinking, combined with evidence of haphazardly parked cars and an ongoing party, for example, could give rise to the risk of potential, future drunk driving incidents, unless the police enter the home and intervene.[7]

Finally, if the police believe that a suspect is in his home and have further reason to believe that he may destroy evidence within the home or flee the scene if not arrested and searched immediately, then the police may be allowed to enter the home due to these risks of destruction of evidence or flight.[8] In all of these cases, of course, the legality of the entry is based largely, if not entirely, on the police officers' account of events, and courts will afford great deference to the officers and their judgment.

Once legally inside, however, the police can't automatically search your home unless they have consent to do so, whether express or implied, from you or in some cases from a third party.

There are, however, other doctrines that allow the police to move forward with a warrantless search. One of these is the protective sweep doctrine, which allows the police to look throughout your home for things or people that could pose a risk or a threat to them. And even if you were arrested outside of the home, the police may still, under certain circumstances, go into the home to look around under the rubric of this protective sweep doctrine.[9]

Another doctrine is the search "incident to arrest" exception. If the police are able to legally get into your home—for example, with your consent, or due to exigent circumstances—and they have a basis to arrest you, they may then conduct a search incident to (or after) your arrest. That means that after you are arrested, the police automatically have the right to search you and parts of your home. This exception to the warrant requirement was originally intended for police safety. Once they decided to arrest you, they should be able to search the immediate area in order to take any weapons to which you might have access, and with which you may harm them. However, this doctrine has been greatly expanded in recent years. Now, even if you are arrested, handcuffed, and are surrounded by officers, the police are still permitted to search the area for weapons (and whatever else they might find) even though it is physically and literally impossible for you to get a weapon and cause them harm. The areas that may be searched in this type of situation even include closed closets, closed containers, and other areas in the immediate vicinity.[10]

Finally, once the police are legally inside your home, they are free to look at anything within plain sight. Should they see (or smell) anything illegal, they are free to seize it and, most likely, expand their search to other parts of the house based on this evidence. At the very least, the evidence they were able to see or smell could give them the legal basis to obtain a search warrant for the remainder of your home.[11]

The warrant requirement certainly isn't what it used to be. And, much like the initial entry into your home, the warrantless police search of your home will be (or will not be) upheld based mostly, if not entirely, on the police officers' testimony. This testimony includes their recollection of their observations and their stated reasons for entering and searching the home.

Chapter 17
Can you make a citizen's arrest?

Yes. In most states you can make a citizen's arrest. However, various issues should be considered before taking such action.

First of all, what is a citizen's arrest? A citizen's arrest is made when a citizen, who is not a member of law enforcement, has directly observed a serious crime being committed and detains the offender until he or she can be turned over to law enforcement. Laws on citizen's arrest may also apply to law enforcement officers when they make arrests outside of their jurisdiction. Nonetheless, definitions of citizen's arrest vary widely from state to state. For example, in some states you may perform a citizen's arrest for even a misdemeanor crime,[1] while in other states you may perform the arrest only if you've witnessed a felony, or if you have good reason to believe that an individual has committed a felony and the felony was in fact committed.[2]

Consider an example: suppose that John is at a local convenience store, picking up some milk. There is one clerk on duty, and she is stocking items at the back of the store. The only customers at the store are John and another young man. John realizes that the young man has reached around the counter at the front end of the store and is taking money from the cash register, which had been left slightly ajar by the distracted clerk. John can see the offender has taken large wads of cash and will soon be out the front door, unnoticed by the clerk. John recalls the phrase "citizen's arrest" and wonders if he could legally detain the offender.

In some states, John would in fact be able to make a citizen's arrest, because he is a United States citizen and he has watched a serious crime take place. (For our purposes, we'll assume that the offense in question constitutes a serious crime, such as felony theft or burglary, but this may not be the case depending on the peculiarities of the particular case.) However, John still needs to weigh several factors before he decides to take action.

First, in which state has this crime taken place? John would have to be familiar with the details of the citizen's arrest law in that state, including the specific procedures for the arrest.[3] If John doesn't follow the state-specific procedures, or if there is no basis for the detainment, he could be sued by the young man, or by the state in a criminal action, for any of several things including false imprisonment.[4]

Second, is John sure that he saw precisely what he thought he saw? In other words, John needs to be convinced that he saw the young man taking wads of cash from the open cash register, and should be sure, for example, that the man was not an out-of-uniform store employee making a routine and legal cash pick up from the drawer. If John is not sure that the action he observed constitutes a serious crime, but executes the citizen's arrest anyway, then John himself could be in trouble. While in some states the citizen's arrest laws protect the citizen in cases of misunderstandings or false accusations, others do not. Therefore, in some cases, if John were to wrongly make a citizen's arrest, he could be liable for making a false accusation against the young man. Again, John could also be accused of crimes himself, such as false imprisonment if he physically detained the young man against his will, or even battery if he physically harmed him during the wrongful arrest.[5]

Third, John should consider the practical consequences of physically detaining the offender, even during a *rightful* citizen's arrest. Even if John does follow the proper procedure but a struggle ensues, he could be found legally liable for charges related to the use of excessive force, even if the offender whom he detained later pleads to, or is found guilty of, the crime for which John detained him.[6]

Fourth, a very crucial matter is John's safety and the safety of others around him. Even if John is sure that he has observed a serious crime, and knows the law and procedure governing a citizen's arrest in his state, he must take his own personal well-being into account before taking action. Of course, John should not make the citizen's arrest if the offender is armed in any way, or seems like a threat to John or to the young clerk in back of the store.[7]

Once John is convinced that a citizen's arrest is the right, legal, and safe thing to do, how might John then go about making the citizen's arrest? As noted, each state has its own clearly specified procedures that need to be followed; nonetheless, the following is a rough outline of the steps that are usually advised.

First, most states would advise John to contact local authorities before, or instead of, taking any action at all, if the situation allows.[8] A citizen's arrest is likely law enforcement's last choice for apprehending a suspected criminal. Second, after contacting authorities, John's likely next step would be to stop the offender and explain that he will be detained by John until police or other law enforcement officials arrive.[9] If John does not "question" the offender as he is detaining him, then John need not recite the *Miranda* warnings to the young man. Third, when the authorities arrive, John's final step would be to inform them of who he is, and precisely what he saw. John would then likely be asked to make a formal, written statement, and may have to testify in court at a later time.[10]

There are a few additional points of interest. A citizen's arrest is different than "shop keeper's privilege," wherein "a merchant has the right to detain a person for a reasonable amount of time and in a reasonable manner if he has a reasonable suspicion that the person shoplifted."[11] Therefore, under some state's laws a person may detain a suspected thief in the person's own establishment if all three criteria of "reasonableness" are met.

Recall that in many cases the person making the citizen's arrest must have also directly observed the crime being committed. Thus, depending on the state, your merely being a Good Samaritan is not sufficient. Suppose, for example, that John is walking down the street, and a woman runs up to him, claiming that her roommate has been stealing from her. John would not be able to go to the woman's apartment to make a citizen's arrest of the roommate, as he did not witness the alleged thefts; additionally, the suspected crimes may not be serious enough to warrant a citizen's arrest.

Consequently, anyone considering a citizen's arrest must be well educated on the specific state's laws, and should proceed with great care and caution.

Criminal Process and Procedure

Chapter 18

Since I'm innocent until proven guilty, will I still have to sit in jail before trial?

Maybe. It depends on whether you can post your bail.

When someone accuses you of a crime, and the prosecutor in your state decides to file a criminal complaint against you, one of the first issues that must be decided is whether you should be released on bond while your case is pending. You will be entitled to a pretrial hearing where a judge, court commissioner, or magistrate will set the terms and conditions of your bond. Most defendants are, in fact, given a bond, which will consist of a monetary condition, commonly referred to as bail, as well as nonmonetary conditions. The non-monetary conditions of bond may consist of any number of things, including an order to appear for all future court dates, to refrain from consuming alcohol and controlled substances, and to avoid certain people or places during the time that your criminal case is pending. If you are released while your case is pending but fail to comply with any of these nonmonetary conditions of bond, your bond could be revoked, your bail could be forfeited, and you could be charged with a separate crime for violating bond.

But what about bail, the monetary part of the bond? If you are innocent until proven guilty, why would you have to pay money, regardless of the amount, to get out of jail? What if you can't afford to pay the amount of bail that is set by the judge? What is to prevent the judge from setting a high bail and keeping you in jail for months, or years, while you wait for your trial date?

The law on bail is governed by the Eighth Amendment to the United States Constitution, which states that "excessive bail shall not be required."[1] In fact, the judge may very well release you on low-cash bail, or on a mere signature or personal recognizance bond. However, the *amount* of your bail generally is *not* related to your guilt or innocence on the underlying charge, nor is it affected by the presumption of innocence.[2] Rather, the purpose of setting bail is, primarily, to ensure that you come to court for all future court dates, including trial.[3] The theory is that if you have to post a lot of bail money, you'll be more likely to show up for trial and less likely to skip town. Why? Because if you show up for court, you'll get your bail money back at the end of the case. (Unless, of course, you are convicted and the judge decides to take some or all of the bail money to pay fines, restitution, or other costs, if there are any.) Conversely, if you were to skip town, your bail would be forfeited and lost forever. Obviously, then, the larger the bail, the more likely you are to stick around and see the case through.

Another purpose of bail is to protect the interests of the community.[4] Here, the theory is that if you have to post a lot of bail money, you'll be more likely to behave properly while you're waiting for your trial date. Why? Because if you don't behave—for example, if you violate a no-drink order or have contact with prohibited parties—your bail could be forfeited, your bond could be revoked, and you could wind up back in jail while you wait for your trial date.

Again, when setting the bail amount, the constitutional requirement is that the bail not be excessive or, conversely stated, that it be reasonable. However, whether bail is excessive or reasonable depends on a number of facts and circumstances, and judges have tremendous leeway in deciding on the proper amount for bail. In fact, bail amounts are highly unpredictable and vary wildly, even for defendants and cases that appear to be quite similar. Given certain facts and circumstances, bail can even be denied, or set extremely high. In that case, if you cannot afford to post the bail amount, you will have to remain in jail while your case is pending.

So what are these facts and circumstances that, in theory at least, are used to determine the *amount* of your bail? The first and primary consideration is flight risk, or the likelihood of your fleeing the jurisdiction instead of sticking around to fight the charges. The higher your flight risk, the higher the judge will set bail. In determining flight risk, the judge will look to several factors.[5] For example, how long have you lived in the community? If you have resided there your entire life, you would be far less likely to flee than if you had just moved there last week. What are your ties to the community? Strong ties mean lower flight risk; if you own a home, have a good job, and have family in the immediate area, those are all factors indicating a low flight risk. What are the nature and number of allegations against you? If you're facing one misdemeanor allegation, you would have little incentive to skip town; however, if you were facing multiple felony counts, your flight risk would go up. Have you ever violated bond conditions or been a fugitive from justice before? If yes, you'll be considered a much higher flight risk, regardless of your community ties and the nature and number of the charges against you.

Second, the judge may also consider other community interests, such as the protection of witnesses, in setting the amount of bail. Some state laws may expressly forbid consideration of such matters when setting bail, stating that such risks should instead be considered when setting the nonmonetary conditions of bond, such as no-contact orders.[6] However, regardless of the language of the law, as a practical matter, these other community interests will be factored into the bail amount. For example, if, when being arrested by police, you scream and repeatedly threaten to kill your accuser, this could be considered a genuine risk to witnesses and the community. Therefore, the community interest here would probably be factored into setting a very high-cash bail. Then, if you cannot post it, the community is safe as you sit harmlessly behind bars. On the other hand, if you do post it, then you have a tremendous incentive to comply with your bond conditions, including the condition that you have no contact with your accuser, or else your bail would be forfeited and your bond revoked.

So, in setting bail, the judge will likely consider your flight risk and other risks that you may pose to the community. However, the judge likely will *not* consider your presumption of innocence, which will instead be an issue for the trial phase of the criminal case.

Chapter 19
Can a child be convicted of a crime?

Yes. And in fact, it's a very common occurrence.

Generally speaking, minors are considered to be juveniles, and when a juvenile is accused of breaking the law, he will be dealt with in the juvenile justice system (juvenile court). This system is separate and distinct from the adult criminal justice system (criminal court), and it focuses more on rehabilitation and less on punishment. However, in some cases, when a juvenile is accused of breaking the law, he can find himself in criminal court. And if he is convicted of a crime, he could be sent to jail, or even to prison. So how can this happen? There are at least three different ways.

First, many states will allow the juvenile to be "waived" out of the juvenile court and into criminal court.[1] Whether the prosecutor can attempt a waiver may depend on the juvenile's age, as well as the crime he is alleged to have committed. Whether the waiver is successful is ultimately up to the judge, who will take into account the same factors, as well as other factors about the juvenile and the facts of the particular case.[2] Often, however, children who are only fourteen or fifteen years old, or even younger, are waived into criminal court and treated as adults.

Second, when a person is accused of wrongdoing, whether the case goes to juvenile court or criminal court may depend *not* on the person's age at the time of the alleged wrongful act, but rather, his age at the time the case is prosecuted.[3] For example, suppose that a fifteen-year-old boy, Johnny, is suspected of stealing a painting from his neighbor's home. However, the neighbors don't make a formal accusation until three years later, and the police subsequently investigate and Johnny is charged with the crime. Because the neighbors waited so long to make the report, Johnny will be charged as an adult in the criminal system.[4] Why? Because Johnny is now eighteen years old, and the key issue is how old he is at the time the case is prosecuted. It doesn't matter how old he was at the time of the alleged wrongful act. Sure, he was only fifteen, and something seems incredibly unjust about prosecuting Johnny and branding him an adult criminal for something he might have done as a child, but that's the way it goes in today's hypervigilant, anticrime climate. We love our punishment, and we love it harsh.

The third way that a juvenile can find himself in the criminal system is that some states have simply changed how they choose to define the terms "juvenile" and "adult." Most of us think of an adult as being twenty-one years old (for purposes of drinking alcohol, for example) or eighteen years old (for purposes of seeing an R-rated movie or staying out past a ten o'clock city curfew, for example). However, some states, when deciding whether a person is sent to juvenile court or adult court, will define "adult" as anyone who has reached the ripe old age of seventeen. For example, if you happened to be a seventeen-year-old Wisconsin resident, you could not legally consume alcohol, buy cigarettes, stay out past curfew, or even consent to having sexual relations. However, if you are accused of wrongful conduct—even conduct that would only give rise to a misdemeanor crime—you are *automatically* considered an adult.[5] No hearing will be held and no waiver is even necessary; you'll be sent straight to adult criminal court.

This system promotes contradictions that should give us pause. For example, suppose that Johnny lives with his parents, and they get into a fight. Johnny gets angry, yells at his mother and father, and breaks an inexpensive vase in the process. The police are called to help calm things down. When they arrive, Johnny's parents, not thinking of the police as agents of the state, tell them what Johnny did. Johnny apologizes, and his parents, seeing that things have calmed down, decide they don't want any more help from the police.

However, regardless of the reason that the police were called, helping Johnny or his family may not be their only concern. Once they become involved and have been told what happened, this is no longer a family matter. But how, exactly, does the state view seventeen-year-old Johnny? Well, on the one hand, he's a juvenile, and because of his age he can't be trusted to make even basic decisions about his own life. For example, he can't be bound by most contracts, he's many years away from being able to have a beer or glass of wine, he can't cast a vote for any political office, and if he were to have sex with, say, an eighteen-year-old girl, he'd be considered a crime victim. These laws, while extreme, obviously reflect the state's view that minors aren't mentally or emotionally developed and need a great deal of protection from themselves and others.

On the other hand, however, when Johnny *acts* like the juvenile that the state says he is, the state may come down hard on him. In this case, because he is seventeen, he will be charged and prosecuted as an adult, in criminal court, with counts of property damage, disorderly conduct, and possibly other crimes as well. In addition, because Johnny damaged property (the vase) belonging to other adult family members with whom he resides (his parents), Johnny could be charged with crimes of domestic violence.[6] Finally, if convicted of *any* crime, he might even have to serve jail time with older, perhaps hardened, prisoners.

Obviously, a double standard is being employed and can certainly lead to extreme consequences with regard to minors in the adult criminal justice system.

Chapter 20
If you accuse someone of a crime, can you later "drop the charges"?

No, absolutely not. When a person reports a crime to the police, and a prosecutor later issues a criminal complaint based on that accusation, the lawsuit is actually between the state (the plaintiff) and the accused individual (the defendant). The person who made the initial accusation (the complaining witness) is *not* a party to the lawsuit, and therefore has no power to drop or dismiss the charges.[1]

You wouldn't know this by watching television, however. Recently on a popular prime-time series, a woman reported to the police that her business partner embezzled $2 million from their company. The police investigated the alleged embezzler, who was subsequently arrested and criminally charged. Yet, the episode ended with the woman's daughter begging her to "drop the charges," and the woman beneficently responding: "I'll consider it." In reality, of course, she would have absolutely no authority or power to do so, as she is not a party to the criminal action.

Although this is only one of many legal issues that television typically gets wrong, the myth that an accuser can "drop the charges" in a criminal case is widespread and particularly problematic in real life. This myth likely developed from the fact that an individual *can* drop or dismiss a complaint in a *civil* case. In a civil case, any individual or legal entity may file a lawsuit against another individual or legal entity in order to settle personal or business matters. Examples of civil lawsuits include actions for breach of contract, personal injury, and disputes over the ownership of land. Some civil causes of action even share the same title as their criminal counterparts, such as battery and false imprisonment, which may have further contributed to the myth.[2]

In these civil cases, the party bringing the suit can indeed decide to "drop the charges." This is because the case is not a criminal one; rather, it is a civil case between two individuals, not between an individual and the state. (The state can, of course, be a party to a civil lawsuit as well, but for our purposes we'll focus on the state's role in bringing criminal charges.) Unlike criminal cases, these civil cases are filed by individual plaintiffs seeking to recover money or some other remedy from another individual. Hence, the plaintiff in a civil case may indeed change her mind regarding the litigation of the case.

For example, you may believe that your neighbor's negligence ruined your expensive collection of antique maps. You want to recover your losses and decide to file a lawsuit against your neighbor for the value of the maps. If you assume that no criminal laws were broken by this accidental damage, such a case would be a purely civil matter. Therefore, it is you, and not your state's prosecutor or district attorney, who files the lawsuit against your neighbor. Before the case goes to court, however, you may have a change of heart for any number of reasons—for example, perhaps you reached a financial settlement, or perhaps you decided you were being too litigious. At this point, you may certainly change your mind and dismiss your civil case.

However, when wrongdoing is reported to the police, the police will refer the matter to the prosecutor's or district attorney's office, which represents the state. In that case, control of the case lies solely with the state, which will often press forward with criminal litigation regardless of the wishes or desires of the complaining witness.

Take, for example, a man who accuses his spouse of domestic violence. Perhaps a shouting match got out of hand and some shoving ensued; the man subsequently called the police complaining that his spouse physically abused him, causing him pain. The police respond to the situation and, being in a "mandatory arrest state,"[3] are forced to arrest the spouse for domestic violence. Now the spouse will sit in jail waiting for the next day's court proceedings, where the prosecutor will file a criminal complaint on behalf of the state.

By this point, however, the complaining witness may regret calling the police. Upon reflection, he thinks that he was probably as much at fault as his spouse. Furthermore, he did not realize the serious repercussions that would flow from his accusations; he and his spouse have a young child together, and he didn't realize that his accusations might take his spouse away from them both for months or even years to come. Furthermore, he is worried about paying legal fees and other costs on behalf of his spouse that will arise as part of this criminal matter that he helped set in motion.

Unlike a civil case, the man in this example has no power or influence to get the charges against his spouse dropped. It is true that he can certainly talk to the prosecutor and express his wishes that the state abandon the criminal case. However, depending on the policies of its office, the prosecutor is not obligated to take these wishes into consideration. Additionally, if the complaining witness went further and attempted to prevent or interfere with the state's prosecution of the criminal case, he could find himself also charged criminally. For example, if he were to recant, minimize, or otherwise change the story that he gave to the police, he could be charged with obstructing an officer—that is, knowingly giving false information to an officer when the officer is performing his official duties—for making the initial police report.[4] Moreover, if the man were called as a witness for the prosecution at his spouse's trial, and his testimony were to contradict his original statement to police, he could be charged with perjury—that is, knowingly making a false material statement under oath in court—based on the change in his story.[5]

Further, even if the complaining witness wanted to "fall on his sword" and do these things for his spouse, he might be surprised to learn that none of this may actually help. For example, if the man were to testify at his spouse's trial that "it was all my fault" and his spouse "did nothing wrong," the prosecutor would introduce into evidence the man's original statement to the police where he said the exact opposite. Due to the change in story, the earlier statement is now legally admissible and would be used to impeach or contradict the man's in-court testimony.[6] The state would further argue that the original story was the accurate one, as the complaining witness is merely changing the story due to the influence exerted by the spouse.

It is quite possible, therefore, that changing the story would do little to help the spouse, and only land the complaining witness in a heap of trouble of his own.

This complaining witness, though hypothetical here, is not unique. In fact, prosecutors and defense lawyers, to their mutual frustration, often hear how a complaining witness wants to "drop the charges." Unfortunately, this myth stems from a misunderstanding of the most basic principles of the criminal court system. Further, it is repeatedly reinforced in our popular culture. All of this, of course, means that this legal myth is likely to persist.

Chapter 21
If you punch someone in a fight, are your hands considered dangerous weapons?

Yes, possibly, depending on the particular state's law and the circumstances surrounding the fight. However, the classification of hands as dangerous weapons is an excellent example of governmental overreaching in the criminal law context.

First, in criminal law, a dangerous weapon can be built in as an element of a particular crime, or it can be a special enhancer that serves to increase the maximum penalty for a crime. For example, the crime of "possessing a firearm in a public building" may require a prosecutor to prove that the defendant possessed a gun while inside a building that is owned or leased by a state governmental body.[1] In this case, the firearm is a *part of* the crime itself. If a defendant did *not* possess a firearm, then he could not have committed this particular crime.

Conversely, sometimes dangerous weapons can be used to enhance particular crimes. For example, the crime of "disorderly conduct" may require a prosecutor to prove that the defendant caused or provoked a disturbance in a public place.[2] In this case, there is no requirement that the defendant possess a firearm or other dangerous weapon; in fact, he could simply be yelling vulgarities, thereby causing a disturbance. However, if he were to commit disorderly conduct by, or while, using a firearm, then he may be convicted of the crime of disorderly conduct, and his maximum penalty may be increased by a specified amount because he was disorderly by, or while, possessing a dangerous weapon.[3]

But before answering our original question—that is, if you

punch someone in a fight can your hands be considered dangerous weapons?—we need first to define the term "dangerous weapon." The example we used above—a firearm—is an obvious example of a dangerous weapon, and few people would debate that. However, many other things may qualify as well. In fact, a dangerous weapon could be defined broadly as anything that is designed as a weapon and has no other legitimate or lawful use. An excellent example of this is brass knuckles, which are designed for one thing and one thing only: to hurt people. But the term "dangerous weapon" is usually defined even *more* broadly and can also include any object that is used or intended to be used to cause serious harm.[4] This definition may include, for example, objects such as an automobile, a kitchen knife, a toaster oven, a remote control, a hairbrush, or virtually any physical object provided it is used or intended to cause serious harm in some fashion. In fact, even the most seemingly innocent objects can qualify. Under certain circumstances, even a pillow can qualify.[5]

But what about your hands? What if you get into a fist fight and win? Can your hands be considered dangerous weapons? Putting aside the issue of self-defense for a moment, some states have answered this question yes, but the result of this decision has caused confusion.

Typically, if you get into a fight and win, the underlying crime with which you may be charged is battery, which would require the prosecutor to prove that you intentionally caused bodily harm to your victim. The use of a dangerous weapon is not required for you to be convicted of this crime. In fact, if you used only your fists, many prosecutors in many states would simply charge you with battery and would not even consider tacking on a dangerous weapon enhancer.

Some courts have said that it is possible for your fists to be considered dangerous weapons, thereby increasing the maximum possible penalty for your crime.[6] This dramatic overreaching, however, is problematic on several levels. First and most obviously, our hands are not objects, devices, or instrumentalities; rather, they are part of our bodies. Second, if our hands are considered to be dangerous weapons, then it would be impossible for anyone to commit a simple battery, that is, causing bodily harm *without* a weapon. Why?

Because our hands, or some body part, are necessary to commit the crime of battery. Therefore, if hands are considered dangerous weapons, then a person could never be convicted of simple battery, because every battery would necessarily have been committed by using a dangerous weapon. This, obviously, would be nonsensical.

But the courts that say hands can be dangerous weapons try to get around this quandary by contending that hands are only *sometimes* dangerous weapons. In other words, it depends on the circumstances of the fight: maybe you used your hands as dangerous weapons, and maybe you didn't. It usually ends up hinging on the level of bodily harm inflicted. For example, if you caused only a simple bruise, then maybe your hands were *not* dangerous weapons. Conversely, if you nearly killed your victim, then maybe your hands *were* dangerous weapons.

The problem with this reasoning, however, is that this "base" has already been covered. That is, nearly every state already has a series of battery or battery-type crimes, ranging from a misdemeanor to the most serious of felonies, which are determined by the level of harm intended or inflicted. For example, the crimes of simple battery, substantial battery, aggravated battery, battery by special circumstances, attempted homicide, and homicide become increasingly harsher based on the level of harm intended by the defendant or actually inflicted on the victim. Therefore, if a person punches someone and causes a bruise, it's a simple battery. If he punches someone and causes great bodily harm, such as brain damage, then it's aggravated battery, a far more serious crime. This does not, however, transform the crime into battery with a dangerous weapon penalty enhancer.[7]

In addition to the basic incompatibility of labeling hands as dangerous weapons, such a classification also leads to some pretty bizarre results. For example, under other laws, a juvenile or an adult on probation may be prevented from possessing dangerous weapons of any kind. This leads to the obvious problem of what such people are to do with their hands. As another example, most jurisdictions prohibit the carrying of concealed weapons, which means, of course, that you'd better not put your hands in your pockets when walking down the street.[8]

Although these examples may be entertaining and extreme, they illustrate the inherent problems with classifying our hands as dangerous weapons.

Your Day in Criminal Court

Chapter 22
Can hearsay be used against you in court?

Yes. And not only can it be used against you in court, but it can also be used by a government prosecutor to convict you of a crime.

First, what is "hearsay"? The formal, legal definition is this:

> Hearsay is a statement, other than one made by the declarant while testifying at the trial or hearing, offered in evidence to prove the truth of the matter asserted.[1]

What? That gibberish means nothing to most of the English-speaking world. In fact, many lawyers and some judges don't even fully understand what it means. So let's break it down with an example. Suppose you've been charged with a crime for allegedly stealing from your roommate, Jennifer. You deny the allegation and demand a jury trial. At trial, however, the state doesn't actually call Jennifer as a witness. Perhaps she won't cooperate, or the prosecutor can no longer locate her or just doesn't want to use her because she'd make a horrible witness. So instead, the prosecutor calls as a witness the police officer to whom Jennifer made her accusation. The police officer takes the witness stand and repeats Jennifer's allegation; specifically, that she saw you taking some of her property without her consent.

Is that hearsay? You bet it is. Using the formal definition, above, the "declarant" of the statement is the person who made it; here, Jennifer. And Jennifer is *not* testifying at trial; rather, the statement is being offered secondhand, through the officer. Finally, the prosecutor is offering the statement to prove the truth of Jennifer's assertion: that *you* took her property without her consent. After all, that's what has to be proved at a trial for theft.

But wait; hearsay is *not* supposed to be admissible! Not only have you heard that mantra a hundred times, but it also makes sense. After all, talk is cheap, and if we were to convict people on hearsay, without the accuser taking the witness stand for cross-examination, then anyone could be convicted for anything. Well, in part, you're right. Here's the general rule regarding the use of hearsay evidence:

> Hearsay is *not* admissible except as provided by these rules or by other rules adopted by the supreme court or by statute.[2]

Sounds good, right? The general rule is that hearsay is *not* admissible. It turns out, however, that there are over thirty—that's right, *thirty*—exceptions to this general rule. With that many exceptions, it doesn't take long to figure out that the exceptions swallow the rule. In fact, the general rule that purports to keep hearsay out of evidence becomes, quite frankly, useless.

Just what are these exceptions? One of the more laughable ones is called the "excited utterance" exception.[3] In our earlier example, if the police officer were simply to testify that, when Jennifer reported the crime, she appeared "excited" or "upset," the law says that even though Jennifer's accusation *is* hearsay, it meets the "excited utterance" exception. Therefore, it *can* be used against you. Why? Because the law is based on the faulty assumption that when someone appears excited or upset, his or her statement carries a guarantee of trustworthiness, and therefore you don't have the need, or the right, to cross-examine the accusation or the accuser.

Even more alarming, prosecutors and police know how easy it is to turn any hearsay accusation into an admissible, excited utterance. All the prosecutor has to do is ask the officer how the "victim" appeared when he or she made the statement, and the officer merely has to reply that he or she appeared "upset," or "excited," and there is no one in the world who can contradict that. It really is that easy.

And if the excited utterance exception doesn't fit the bill, there are other hearsay exceptions available to the prosecutor. For example, there is the "present sense impression exception" that allows into evidence any statements that are made immediately after the event in question.[4] There is also the "then existing mental, emotional or physical condition exception" that allows into evidence any statements that describe pain, fear, or some other emotional or physical state of being.[5] Either of these exceptions will serve the purpose and will get the statements into evidence. Amazingly, there's even a "catch-all exception" if the prosecutor can't somehow squeeze the hearsay through one of the other thirty-plus exceptions. In other words, if a prosecutor wants to get hearsay into evidence against you, he can do it.

Can it be that easy to convict someone of a crime? In theory, it shouldn't be. The United States Constitution, as well as the individual state constitutions, guarantees each and every one of us the right of confrontation; that is, the right to cross-examine our accusers.[6] Unfortunately, this right of confrontation is as easy to bypass as the hearsay rule, and in reality is nothing more than a minor speed bump for a prosecutor intent on conviction.

Our United States Supreme Court recently held that the right of confrontation applies to only certain hearsay statements known as "testimonial" hearsay.[7] In other words, if the hearsay statement—in our case, Jennifer's statement that *you* stole from her—was obtained by police in their efforts to investigate a crime, it will be "testimonial" and *cannot* be used against you. Conversely, if the police obtained the statement for any other purpose, such as assessing the situation or rendering aid to Jennifer, then the hearsay is *not* testimonial, and you *don't* have any right of confrontation. In that case, the police officer *may* repeat the accuser's words at trial, and the jury may convict you if they so please.

But how does the judge decide whether the hearsay is testimonial or not? The same way that he decides whether the accuser was "excited" when making her accusation: the police officer will tell him. All the officer has to do is testify that he asked Jennifer what happened, *not* for the purpose of investigating a crime but rather because Jennifer appeared "upset." Therefore, he was merely trying to assess the situation to see if Jennifer needed any assistance. That is all the officer needs to say. In one fell swoop the officer and the prosecutor dispense with the general rule on hearsay as well as the Confrontation Clause of the United States Constitution.[8]

So, in reality, not only can hearsay be used in court, but it can be used much of the time, and can even be used to convict you of a crime without giving you any opportunity to cross-examine your accuser or the accusation against you.

Chapter 23

Does a speedy trial mean you'll get your trial within six months?

Absolutely not. What about a year? Two years? Three years? The answer is: none of the above.

When a defendant is charged with a crime, he has numerous constitutional rights, including the constitutional right to a speedy trial.[1] Most defendants, however, are surprised to learn that "speedy" doesn't really mean "speedy." In fact, in some cases the prosecutor can take up to three, four, or even five years to try your case.

First of all, it's important to distinguish the constitutional right to a speedy trial from other speedy trial rights. Speedy trial rights can be found all over the place in criminal law. The sources of these various rights include federal law for federal criminal cases, the interstate agreement on detainers, various state statutes, and various local court rules. However, these nonconstitutional rights either apply to relatively few of the total number of criminal cases, or, in some cases, have no real remedy if they are violated. Therefore, the topic of this chapter is devoted to the *constitutional* right to a speedy trial.

The constitutional right not only applies, in theory, to every criminal case, but it also seems to have some teeth to it. That is, if you are charged with a crime and your speedy trial right is violated, your case will then get dismissed "with prejudice," meaning that the prosecutor cannot refile the case against you. So then, under the right to a speedy trial, how long do the prosecutor and the judge have to get your case to trial before you're entitled to a dismissal? Well, it could be many, many years. In fact, there's no firm time limit at all. Rather, it comes down to a four-factor balancing test, and the court is allowed to weigh and balance the factors in any way it wishes.[2]

Here's how it works: Suppose you're arrested for a crime on May 1 and you're released and issued a summons to appear in court on July 1. You go through all the various court hearings, and you get your first scheduled trial date on November 1. However, when it comes time for trial, there are many, many other defendants appearing in court for trial that same day, which is common. The judge and prosecutor decide to try a case other than yours, and your case gets adjourned to February 1 of the following year. Come February 1, however, the same thing happens, and your case is adjourned to May 1. Come May 1, you and your lawyer are, once again, ready for trial, and so is the court. This time, however, the prosecutor forgot to subpoena a key witness, and he requests, and receives, another adjournment, which means another delay. Your trial date is now set for August 1, about one year and three months after you were first arrested.

Does your case have to be dismissed? Probably not. Remember, there is no firm time limit that has to be followed; instead, the court will analyze and balance four factors, which are: (1) the length of the delay; (2) the reason for the delay; (3) whether you demanded a speedy trial; and (4) whether you suffered prejudice as a result of the delay.[3]

Here's how the court will probably balance the factors in your case: First, the delay is only one year and three months. (That's right, "only.") The court may very well find that this is common in its jurisdiction, and therefore analysis of the other factors is not even necessary.[4] However, in most cases, a delay of more than one year will force the court to at least look at the other factors. Second, the *reason* for the delay is due to court congestion for the first two adjournments, and the prosecutor's failing to subpoena a witness for the last adjournment. You might think this would weigh heavily in your favor, as neither of those reasons is your fault, but you'd probably be wrong. While the judge may find that the delay should be attributed to the court and the prosecutor, he will also find that none of the delay was *intentional*.[5] In other words, the court can't control the congestion, and the prosecutor's failure to subpoena a witness was probably only negligent rather than intentional. Therefore, all may be forgiven. Third, you may never have formally *demanded* a speedy trial. If you had done so, that factor would weigh in your favor. However, if you did not make the formal demand, chalk another one up for the prosecutor.[6] Fourth, unless one of your key witnesses has disappeared, you probably haven't suffered any real *prejudice* as a result of the delay, at least not in the eyes of the court. Sure, you've been living under restrictive bond conditions for over a year, and you've had the anxiety of a criminal case hanging over your head. However, this type of prejudice is not very quantifiable or verifiable in most cases and is seen as simply an ordinary part of our justice system.[7]

So, there you have it. Despite the year-plus delay, your constitutional right to a speedy trial almost certainly has *not* been violated. And even if more factors had been in your favor, the chances are you'd still lose. Why? Because a court can simply give the other factors—for example, the fact that you weren't prejudiced by the delay—more weight in the balancing test. In fact, in some cases, delays of three, four, or five years have been tolerated under the court's four-factor balancing test.[8]

The constitutional right to a speedy trial, like most constitutional rights, is not a firm, bright-line rule. Rather, it is a vague, factor-laden test that is subject to a tremendous amount of discretion and, in some cases, manipulation by the courts.

Chapter 24
Can you be convicted of a crime for a mistake or an accident?

Yes, in many cases you can be.

When most people think of "criminals" and "crimes," they think of bad people out in the community doing dreadful things. Classic examples include, of course, armed robbery, burglary, rape, and murder, to name only a few of the crimes we've all heard about and have seen played out as central themes in movies and television shows. Further, all of these crimes have something in common: In each case, the bad guy is *intentionally* doing something that he knows is morally wrong. As a result, if the perpetrator is arrested, prosecuted, and convicted, it makes sense to most of us that he be criminally punished, including a possible jail or prison sentence.

Conversely, it may also make sense that people who made a mistake or were involved in accidents should *not* be criminally punished. That's not to say that these people shouldn't be liable for what they've done, of course. After all, that's what the civil law system, as opposed to the criminal law system, is for. For example, if a driver causes a car accident, the driver could be liable to the injured party in a civil suit and may have to pay money for hospital bills, property damage to the car, and even the dreaded punitive damages. But it wouldn't sit right with most of us if the negligent driver was also charged criminally by the state for battery and property damage. It just doesn't fit our common view of what the criminal justice system should be.

Surprisingly, however, not all crimes require bad intent, or what lawyers call the "guilty mind," or *mens rea*. In fact, crimes of recklessness, negligence, and strict liability have exploded over the years, as our government continues to criminalize more and more of our behavior. Whether someone can be convicted of a crime *without* having intended to do anything wrong or harmful will depend on a number of factors and varies widely from state to state, crime to crime, and statute to statute.

This issue is sometimes framed in terms of a "knowledge" requirement. Knowledge, in this sense, doesn't mean knowledge of the law. In fact, we can all be convicted of a law we've never even heard of and never even dreamed existed. Here, the age-old maxim holds true: ignorance of the law is no excuse for breaking it. But often, in order to be convicted of a crime, the state would have to prove that a defendant had knowledge of a certain fact or facts. Let's look at an example, starting with the crime of possession of marijuana:

> Whoever possesses a substance that is marijuana, *and so possesses the substance knowing or believing that it is a controlled substance of any kind*, is guilty of a misdemeanor or, if it is the person's second or subsequent offense, a felony.[1]

In other words, in order to convict a defendant for possessing marijuana, the state would have to prove that he or she *knowingly* possessed marijuana, or at least knowingly possessed a substance believing that it was an illegal substance of some kind. Under this statute, therefore, some cases of possession would *not* constitute a crime. For example, if a defendant borrows his friend's jacket and, unbeknownst to the defendant, that jacket has marijuana in the pocket, he would *not* be guilty of criminal possession. Sure, the defendant possessed the marijuana, but not *knowingly*. Therefore, he should not be convicted. That makes sense.

But some crimes don't require that the state prove this knowledge element. Consider, for example, the crime of misdemeanor sexual assault, which may typically read as follows:

> Whoever has sexual contact with another person, including the touching of another person's breast or buttocks, without the consent of that person, is guilty of misdemeanor sexual assault.[2]

A big difference in this statute, when compared to the marijuana statute, is that to convict a defendant of sexual assault, all the prosecutor has to prove is that the victim did not consent to the touching. It doesn't matter one bit that the defendant believed the victim consented, or even had *good reason* to believe that the victim —an adult—consented. As a result, under this statute, defendants have been convicted of sexual assault for simply touching their victim, even when their victim was fully alert and conscious, was not threatened by the defendant in any way, knew the defendant well, never told the defendant "no" or "stop," and even had a prior sexual history with the defendant. In other words, the prosecutor would *not* have to prove that the defendant *knew* the touching was without consent; further, the victim was under no obligation to communicate his or her *lack* of consent to the defendant.

Other times, however, this issue is framed not in terms of the knowledge requirement, but rather in terms of a "mistake" defense. Let's look at another example, this time starting with the crime of trespass:

> Whoever intentionally enters the dwelling of another without consent, and provokes a breach of the peace, is guilty of criminal trespass. An honest mistake of fact, if it negates the essential state of mind, is a defense to criminal liability.[3]

In other words, a mistake of fact could be a defense. If, for example, a defendant is invited over to a friend's apartment but mistakenly walks into the neighboring apartment and scares the living daylights out of those people, the defendant's conduct would appear to be criminal. After all, he intentionally entered another's dwelling without consent and provoked a breach of the peace. However, in this case, the defendant could assert the mistake defense. That is, the defendant could argue that he was simply mistaken as to the apartment number and had no bad intent whatsoever. Under these facts, the defendant should not be convicted of a crime.

But some statutes don't allow a mistake defense. And many of these statutes have the most severe penalties and the largest impact on a defendant's life. Consider, for example, the so-called statutory rape crimes, which may typically read as follows:

Whoever has sexual contact with a person who has not attained the age of 18 years is guilty of sexual assault of a child. *A mistake as to the age of the minor is not a defense.*[4]

Under this law, if the prosecutor proved that the defendant had sexual contact with a minor, the defendant would be convicted, period. It wouldn't matter that the minor agreed to the sexual contact, nor would it matter one bit that the defendant was *mistaken* as to the minor's age. In fact, the defendant may have truly believed that the minor was actually an adult, and may even have had good reason to believe that. Even if the minor had a fake ID card good enough to fool the doorman at a night club, the law still says that the defendant cannot rely on his mistake of the minor's age as a defense. Instead, the defendant will be convicted.

In addition to "knowledge" and "mistake" issues, the problem can also be framed in terms of "intent." For example, a battery crime will usually require the prosecutor to prove that a defendant not only caused harm to another, but also intended to cause him harm.[5] Therefore, accidentally bumping into someone and knocking that person over would *not* be a crime, even if the person is injured in the process. Likewise, a criminal property damage statute will usually require the prosecutor to prove that a defendant not only damaged another's property but also intended to damage the property.[6] Therefore, accidentally knocking too hard on an old glass door and breaking it would *not* be a crime, despite the very real property damage that occurred.

Nonetheless, a person can be guilty of a crime—even a very serious felony crime—when she had no bad intent whatsoever. For example, a person who causes even a slight amount of harm, including only temporary and mild pain, can be convicted of a felony if found to be "reckless,"[7] or even just "negligent."[8] A person can also be guilty of a crime by omission—that is, by failing to take action where the law requires her to do so—in certain circumstances. This would include legally imposed obligations with regard to children.[9] Finally, and most alarmingly, a person can also be convicted for the acts of another person—a concept known as "vicarious liability"—even if the person didn't take part in, or even know about, the wrongful acts or conduct. This type of liability most commonly occurs in the context of corporate or white-collar crime.[10]

Many justifications for these extremely broad criminal statutes have been offered, but the bottom line is that our multiple layers of government—whether federal, state, local, administrative, or otherwise—continue to expand laws and encroach on our freedoms. Our collective desire to regulate conduct and our lust to punish people, even when we are initially reasonable and well-intentioned, often prevents us from using claims of "lack of bad intent," "lack of knowledge," "mistake," or "accident" in our own defense.

Chapter 25
Can you be convicted of multiple crimes for a single act?

Yes, without a doubt, and despite any notions you may have about "double jeopardy" protection.

Consider a very common scenario that forms the basis for countless domestic violence prosecutions across our nation. Suppose you are arguing with your spouse, and he has had enough and tries to leave the room. You decide, however, that you're not finished arguing, and you grab your spouse's arm to keep him from leaving. This goes on for a minute or two, and due to ill will, hot heads, and a lot of alcohol being consumed by both of you, your spouse decides to call the police. When the police eventually refer the case to the prosecutor's office, and you are ultimately charged criminally, the formal, criminal complaint against you reads as follows:

> . . . Spouse and Defendant argued, at which time Spouse tried to leave the room. Defendant, however, did not stop arguing, and grabbed Spouse's upper arm to prevent spouse from leaving. Spouse was held in that position for approximately two minutes, at which time Defendant continued to argue and yell at Spouse. Spouse reported that this not only caused pain, but was also against Spouse's will and without consent. Officer Friendly photographed Spouse's arm, which showed signs of bruising on the upper part of the arm where Defendant grabbed and restrained Spouse . . .

Although there are two sides to every story, and you feel you didn't do anything that you would consider "criminal," you really don't dispute the factual allegations. You also recognize that, if you both hadn't been drinking, cooler heads probably would have prevailed and you would have let your spouse walk away from the argument. Much to your surprise, however, you find yourself charged with *three* different crimes for the single act of grabbing your spouse's arm. What are these charges? *Disorderly conduct* for causing a disturbance,[1] *battery* for causing physical pain without your spouse's consent,[2] and *felony false imprisonment* for detaining your spouse against his will.[3] And all for the single act of grabbing your spouse's arm.

But what about double jeopardy protection? How can you possibly be charged with *three* crimes for doing *one* thing? That's a good, and very logical, objection. And the Constitution *does* promise that "nor shall any person be subject for the same offense to be twice put in jeopardy[.]"[4] But the funny thing about the Constitution is that, after many years of Supreme Court case decisions, the Constitution doesn't mean what the Constitution says; rather, it means what the Supreme Court says. And the Supreme Court says that as long as the crimes with which you are charged are sufficiently different from each other, then you can be charged and convicted of all of them.[5] Sure, the prosecutor couldn't charge you with three counts of, say, battery for your single act; however, disorderly conduct, battery, and false imprisonment are all different from each other, therefore it is okay to charge these three crimes for a single act.

But how are those three crimes different if they are all based on the same act of grabbing your spouse's arm? Disorderly conduct requires, among other things, that your conduct "disturbed" your spouse, while battery and false imprisonment do not. Conversely, battery requires that your conduct caused your spouse "pain or injury," while disorderly conduct and false imprisonment do not. Finally, false imprisonment requires that you "confine or restrain" your spouse against his will, no matter how briefly, while disorderly conduct and battery do not. Therefore, because each crime has a component, or element, that the others do not, you can be charged, and possibly convicted, of all three. And not only that, but if convicted you could receive *consecutive* sentences on all three, that is, sentences that run one after another, rather than at the same time.

How's that for being put in jeopardy twice (or rather, thrice) for the same offense?

But it gets even worse. It actually turns out that you *can* be charged, and convicted, of several counts of the *exact same crime* for a single act.[6] Consider this example: suppose you're driving a car and going too fast around a corner. You lose control for a split second but quickly regain it and no one is hurt. Unfortunately for you, however, there are a number of witnesses to your bad driving, including a police officer. You're pulled over and ultimately charged with *seven* counts of the same statute: felony second-degree reckless endangerment of safety.[7]

How can this be? Simple. In addition to being able to charge you with several *different* crimes for the *same* act, the government can also charge you with *multiple* counts of the *same* crime, as long as there are *different* victims. But, you wisely point out, there were no victims in the driving example discussed above; after all, no one was hurt by the car. No harm, no foul, right? Not so fast. The term "victim" doesn't really mean what you and I think it means; rather, it means whatever the legislature says. And the legislature says that "victim," in this case, means every single person who was put at risk of *potential* injury by your driving. By these standards, any person in the area is a victim, and that's another count against you. In our example, there were seven people, and that's seven counts.

So, double jeopardy protection isn't all it's cracked up to be. And just think if you had driven recklessly immediately after you argued with your spouse. Then, you would find yourself charged with ten crimes all in a span of ten minutes. Now that's a bad day.

Chapter 26
Can you be convicted of a crime without any evidence?

Yes. That is, if you define "evidence" as something *more* than a mere allegation. In that case, then yes, you *can* be convicted without evidence, and based solely on an allegation of wrongdoing. However, criminal courts define the term "evidence" to include the allegation itself. So as far as the law is concerned, if you are convicted based solely on an allegation, you *are* being convicted based on evidence.[1]

Here's a great example: A defendant was accused of child sexual assault, the most serious felony this side of first-degree murder. The child testified at trial that he went to bed around eleven, and around midnight the defendant had sexual contact with him. When asked how he knew it happened at midnight, he testified that he never looked at a clock, but rather that he just knew. When asked at what time he woke up prior to or during the assault, he testified that he *never* woke up. Rather, he slept the entire time from when he went to bed until waking up the next morning. But the child testified that he knew this assault wasn't a dream because, he said, "I had a different dream when I was sleeping."[2]

No other evidence of any kind, whether physical evidence or testimony, was presented by the state. The state then rested and the case went to the jury. The defense could have put on its own evidence and pointed out how the child previously gave statements of the alleged crime that were inconsistent with his in-court testimony. However, as the court acknowledged, "[p]resenting *any* defense carries the risk of having the jury reject the defense rather than focusing on the weakness of the State's case."[3]

And, as the court implied, the state's case was incredibly weak. An alleged victim saying that he was assaulted, even though he was asleep, never woke up, and had other dreams that night, shouldn't strike a rational person as proof, let alone proof beyond all reasonable doubt. The defense probably grew even more confident given that no one else in the house witnessed any such crime, and there was no physical evidence at all. Rather, there was only an allegation, and a highly implausible one at that.

Despite this, however, the defendant was convicted of felony sexual assault of a child, which is one of the most serious crimes, with perhaps the most draconian punishments and collateral consequences of any crime, other than first-degree murder. The defendant appealed but lost.[4] What's surprising, however, is that when he appealed, he wasn't even allowed to challenge the sufficiency of the evidence on which the jury based its verdict of guilt. Why not? Because the evidence, which includes testimony of witnesses, is to be evaluated and judged solely by the jury. The court could only step in if the testimony itself was insufficient to constitute a crime.

For example, if a child were to testify that the defendant touched him on his foot, and the jury convicted the defendant of sexual assault of a child, the appellate court could overrule the verdict. Why? Because touching a foot cannot, under any circumstance, constitute a sexual assault. However, if a child were to testify that the defendant touched "his privates," even if the child admitted to sleeping the entire time and dreaming other dreams, and the jury convicted the defendant of sexual assault of a child, the appellate court cannot overrule that verdict. Why not? Because credibility determinations are left entirely to the jury. If a jury is convinced of guilt, then nothing further can be done.

And, not only can a person be convicted on a mere allegation, but the accuser, whether an adult or a child and regardless of the nature of the accusation, often doesn't even have to testify in court. Instead, someone else can simply take the witness stand and repeat what she claims the accuser said to her. The accuser's alleged statement gets into evidence without any oath that it is truthful, and without any cross-examination of the accuser. This happens because there are about thirty exceptions to the hearsay rule, and our constitutional right of confrontation has become incredibly watered-down.[5] For these reasons, the state can often bypass the alleged victim altogether and instead call to the witness stand a person who allegedly heard the allegation at some previous time. This person could be a 911 operator,[6] a nurse,[7] a police officer,[8] or anyone else who claims to have heard what the alleged victim said.

So, in sum, you *can* be convicted without evidence, based on a mere allegation, and the state may not even have to call your accuser to testify under oath. Therefore, if you find yourself accused of a serious crime, give serious thought to plea bargaining before forging ahead to a jury trial.

Chapter 27
If a jury convicts you of a crime, can you appeal the verdict?

Yes . . . sort of. We've all heard the famous threat from convicted defendants: "I'll appeal this conviction all the way to the Supreme Court!" But how realistic is this?

First, the vast majority of criminal cases are prosecuted in the courts of our fifty states and not in our federal courts. There are, of course, federal criminal laws and federal criminal cases. However, these cases are extremely small in number when compared to all of the cases prosecuted in our numerous state courts.

Second, in most cases, a criminal defendant who has been convicted of a crime does get an appeal as a matter of right. However, the appeal is not to the United States Supreme Court; instead, the appeal is to the state appellate court in the same state where the defendant was convicted. It is possible, but not common, for a defendant to "jump" court systems. Under certain limited circumstances a defendant convicted of a crime in a state court can work his way into the federal court system, including a federal circuit court of appeal or even the United States Supreme Court.[1] For our purposes, however, we'll focus on the far more common scenario: a defendant is convicted of a crime in state court and then appeals to the state's appellate court.

The next question, then, is on what basis can a defendant appeal his conviction? Let's look at a hypothetical example. Suppose your neighbor falsely accused you of battering him the last time you two argued during your ongoing property-line dispute. Your neighbor reported this to the police, who reported it to the state's district attorney in your county, who then filed a criminal complaint and prosecuted you for battery and disorderly conduct. However, you knew the allegations were false and you were confident that you would be found not guilty. Therefore, you chose to take the case to a jury trial rather than take a plea bargain for something you didn't even do. You viewed this case as a battle between you and your neighbor, and there's no way you were going to back down. (In reality, however, this was a criminal case and the parties to it were the state, represented by the prosecutor or the district attorney, and you. Your neighbor, the alleged victim, was only a complaining witness, not a party to the action.)

In any event, the case went to trial, where your neighbor was called by the prosecutor as a witness. And even though your neighbor had no injuries, and there were no other witnesses to your alleged battery, the jury convicted you. You, of course, are outraged at the injustice and demand an appeal. However, when you visit an appellate lawyer—or when he visits you, if you've been sentenced to jail or prison—he tells you that while you have the *right* to appeal, you can't just appeal for any old reason. Instead, you must have some legal *basis* for an appeal.[2]

Appellate judges don't (and can't) review a case to see if they think the jury made the right decision. As we learned in the previous chapter—"Can you be convicted of a crime without any evidence?"—a jury's guilty verdict is virtually unchallengeable, in and of itself. As a general but firm rule, an appellate court cannot overturn an "incorrect" verdict even if it wanted to do so. Even when a defendant is accused of a crime with no witnesses, no physical evidence, and an incredibly implausible story, the jury is free to convict if they want to,[3] and for any reason they deem fit, including legally improper reasons such as the race or national origin of the defendant. If a juror were to come forward with such allegations against a fellow juror *during* a trial or *during* jury deliberations, a mistrial might be granted. However, for the most part, there is no supervision of a jury. As a practical matter, then, jurors can do whatever they please.

Instead, a legal basis for appeal usually involves a mistake in procedure rather than lack of evidence or questionable jury verdicts. For example, let's go back to your hypothetical battery case against your neighbor. If there was a mistake in procedure at your trial, and you didn't receive your day in court, so to speak, then it is possible that you can win your appeal. What is a mistake in procedure? Most commonly, someone screwed up. For example, the judge may have made a horrible decision during your trial. Maybe he allowed the prosecutor to tell the jury how you have a reputation for being an aggressive hothead, something that clearly is *inadmissible* character evidence.[4] Or maybe he prevented your lawyer from telling the jury how your neighbor was just convicted of perjury, and therefore he is a liar who can't be trusted, something that clearly is *admissible* evidence.[5] Any of these judicial errors could be considered a mistake in procedure and could serve as the legal basis for an appeal.

But there are other types of mistakes in procedure. As another example, the prosecutor may have committed misconduct at some point in the proceedings. Maybe he never disclosed the written statement of another neighbor, who claims to have seen the whole thing and told the police that you never laid a hand on the alleged victim.[6] Or maybe the prosecutor made improper arguments to the jury— arguments based on improper factors such as your race, religion, or national origin.[7] Any such prosecutorial misconduct could be considered a mistake in procedure and could also serve as the basis for an appeal.

As a final example, your own trial attorney may have, at some point during your case, made a mistake that resulted in you receiving *ineffective* assistance of counsel, which would violate your constitutional right to have an effective attorney.[8] Maybe he knew about the favorable eyewitness but never bothered to call him as a witness. Maybe he knew of prior, inconsistent stories that the alleged victim told the police but never confronted or cross-examined him at trial with those prior statements. Again, these errors could also be used as a possible basis for an appeal.

While there is a good chance that someone—the judge, prosecutor, or your defense lawyer—screwed up at some point during the case, don't get too excited just yet. The courts have developed something called the "harmless error" doctrine. A skeptical view of this doctrine is that it was designed to uphold convictions, no matter how many errors were made at trial. The doctrine works this way: even when *everyone* made errors in your trial—the trial judge, the prosecutor, *and* your own defense lawyer—appellate judges can simply look at your case and decide that, even had these people *not* made the errors, you *still* would have been convicted. Therefore, their errors were "harmless," and the jury's guilty verdict will be upheld.[9]

But the prospect of appealing your conviction gets even grimmer. Not only do you have to find a very specific error on which to hang your hat, and not only do you have to argue that the error was *not* harmless, but even if you were to win, winning isn't all it's cracked up to be. First, even if you win your appeal—a rare event, indeed—you usually don't walk free with an acquittal. Instead, the prosecutor gets a second kick at the cat, and your case gets set for a second trial where the prosecutor will try to convict you again. This time, however, he'll try to convict you without the errors that occurred in the first trial.[10]

Second, if the prosecutor wins again and you get convicted a second time, you better watch out. Why? Because the judge can give you a stiffer sentence than the one he gave you after the first conviction. In theory, judges should not do this to punish you because you exercised your right to appeal your conviction, and won. Instead, they have to give a reason or a new factor to support their harsher sentence the second time around. And if a judge is able to do that, then he can legally increase your punishment and make things worse than if you had never appealed in the first place.[11]

What's the lesson in all of this? The lesson is twofold. First, if you're appealing your conviction, it's really tough to get what you wish for: a new trial. And, if you get a new trial, you might even be sorry that you wished for it.

Chapter 28
Can you beat your case by claiming you're insane?

Probably not.

Many television programs and movies about the criminal justice system give us the impression that it's easy to commit a crime—say, murder—and then "get off" by claiming insanity. Hollywood loves to create the image of a crafty defendant who dupes the legal system and then walks away scot-free. (In the end, however, some form of "rough justice" usually prevails and the defendant gets what is coming to him.) In reality, however, using the insanity defense is far more difficult, if not impossible. Further, even if a defendant were successful with an insanity defense, the repercussions can be just as serious, or even more serious, than they would be with a straight criminal conviction.

The law on insanity, like many of our laws, varies greatly from state to state. In fact, some states may not even allow the insanity defense under any set of circumstances.[1] In addition, the concept of insanity is often confused with other, closely related mental health issues. Generally speaking, there are at least two (and probably three) different types of mental health issues in a criminal case. The first one is competence.

Every defendant must be competent before the state can proceed with criminal charges against him. Competency has nothing to do with the defendant's state of mind at the time he allegedly committed the crime. Rather, it has to do with his state of mind *now*, at the present time. In other words, when the defendant comes into court for a court hearing, he has to be able to generally understand what is going on around him, why he is there, and who the different people are in the courtroom, such as the judge, the defense lawyer, and the prosecutor. If a defendant is so mentally ill that he cannot understand these basic concepts, then he is unable to assist in his defense, is not competent, and the case may not proceed against him until he becomes competent.[2]

Once there is some hint of incompetence—for example, if the defendant can't communicate with his lawyer or behaves bizarrely in the courtroom—anyone involved in the case, including the prosecutor or the judge, can raise the issue of competence. In fact, if the defense lawyer has reason to believe his client is incompetent, he may be legally *obligated* to raise the issue. Once the issue is raised, the court may appoint a medical professional to evaluate the defendant and give an opinion as to his competency to proceed.[3] It is the rare case, indeed, where a defendant is found to be incompetent. Generally, even mentally disabled and mentally ill individuals can be declared competent, and the criminal case against them will move forward. And even in the rare case that a defendant is found to be incompetent, the criminal case against him doesn't just go away. Further, even if the criminal case were to be dismissed, the defendant would likely be facing a mental commitment where he would be placed into the state's custody anyway.[4]

Assuming the defendant is competent to proceed, however, the next mental responsibility issue is the insanity defense at trial. The issue of sanity, unlike the issue of competence, deals with the defendant's mental state at the time he allegedly committed the crime. (Interestingly, it is therefore possible to both be insane and incompetent, since each deals with a different point in time.) Contrary to numerous references in our popular culture, to prevail on the insanity defense is either impossible (because some states won't permit its use under any circumstances) or extremely difficult (because the cards have purposely been stacked against the defendant).[5]

The way it works is this: if the defendant pleads guilty to, or is found guilty of, the underlying charge or charges against him, then he can still litigate the issue of mental responsibility, or insanity. Suppose a defendant is charged with disorderly conduct and unlawful use of a telephone for threatening people who had previously called him on his home telephone. The defendant may choose to plead guilty to the crimes but demand a jury trial to determine the mental responsibility issue. In other words, he could argue that, even though he made the threats that constituted the crimes, he shouldn't be held accountable in the criminal justice system. Rather, he may argue that he was mentally ill, and either didn't know what he was doing was wrong or simply wasn't able to control his own conduct.

In order to prevail on the insanity defense, the defendant will likely need to call expert medical witnesses who have evaluated him and will testify in support of his mental disease or defect, as well as his inability to conform his conduct to the law or to appreciate right from wrong.[6] The prosecutor, who will be opposing this defense, may have his own experts who will say the opposite of the defendant's experts. In some cases, the courts will put very strict constraints on the defendant's ability to use evidence in support of his defense.[7] Further, juries, perhaps in fear of being duped, or perhaps feeling the defendant deserves punishment whether or not he is actually insane, may simply reject an insanity defense. Often, the best chance of succeeding on such a defense will be where the defendant's actions didn't cause any actual harm and weren't motivated to gain something of value. For example, winning an insanity trial on charges of murder (where actual harm was inflicted) or of burglary (where the defendant benefited financially from the crime) might prove to be very difficult. However, if the defendant's crime was limited to threatening other people, and that crime caused no physical harm, had no apparent motive, and brought no financial benefit to the defendant, the jury may be far more open to considering issues of mental illness and ultimately finding the defendant insane.

Going back to our disorderly conduct and telephone harassment example, if the defendant could show that he had a mental disease or defect that kept him from either conforming his behavior to the law or appreciating the wrongfulness of his conduct, then he might prevail in his insanity defense at trial. However, recall that he would have already been found guilty on the underlying crimes, either by a plea or by a verdict. Therefore, even if he wins the insanity phase of his trial, he doesn't just get to walk off scot-free. Instead, he will be found not guilty *by reason of insanity* (or by reason of mental disease or defect) and will be committed to the custody of the state.[8]

This postverdict commitment could be in the form of an in-patient commitment at an institution, or out-patient commitment with frequent monitoring. The form of the commitment depends on a number of factors, including the nature of the defendant's acts as well as the treatment options available "on the outside." In some cases, and for some crimes, a defendant found not guilty by reason of insanity may be worse off than if he had simply been convicted of the crimes. For example, if convicted (as a sane person) of disorderly conduct or unlawful use of a telephone, the defendant may simply receive probation, a fine, or a short jail term. On the other hand, if the defendant is found not guilty by reason of insanity, the manda-tory commitment will follow. In some ways, and in some cases, this commitment could be a greater punishment than the fine, the pro-bation, or the short jail term.

Chapter 29
If you're charged with a crime, can you represent yourself in court?

Probably. But it's a lengthy process to get to that point.

First, when a citizen is charged with a crime, he has many constitutional rights. Some of these rights, such as the right of confrontation and cross-examination, are malleable and flexible, and can easily be bypassed by a skilled prosecutor or a state-leaning judge.[1] Other rights, however, are nearly absolute. These include, for example, the right to trial by jury and the right to testify on one's own behalf at trial. Other constitutional rights include the right to the effective assistance of an attorney. But what about the right to go to trial alone, *without* an attorney? This may, at first, seem like an odd request. To use an analogy, what patient would want to perform his own surgery, without the benefit of a surgeon? Surprisingly, many defendants think they know better than their lawyer, and therefore want to fully represent themselves at trial, in addition to testifying at their own trial.

Despite the age-old saying that a lawyer who represents himself has a fool for a client, even a nonlawyer has the right to represent himself at trial.[2] This right, however, is not absolute; in fact, the trial judge may go through several highly subjective steps before allowing the defendant to proceed to trial *pro se*, that is, without an attorney. First, the request for self-representation may actually trigger the most basic of inquiries: whether the defendant is mentally competent to stand trial, regardless of whether he has an attorney or goes it alone. Essentially, the judge may inquire as to whether the defendant fully understands the nature of the proceedings, the role of the different "players" in the courtroom, and the consequences of a criminal conviction.[3] If there is any doubt, the judge may refer the defendant to a medical professional who will offer an expert opinion as to whether the defendant is competent to stand trial.[4]

Second, assuming the defendant has this very basic level of competence, the judge may then try to determine, through more questioning, whether the defendant understands his constitutional right to, and the importance of, a lawyer. In other words, the judge will want to make sure that the defendant understands the value of what he is giving up, and the risks that he faces by going to trial without a lawyer. Finally, the judge will also make certain that the defendant not only understands the right to counsel, but also that he chooses to relinquish the right freely and voluntarily.[5]

This stage is actually a very important one. In fact, the judge may spend a great deal of time questioning the defendant on this matter, not because he particularly cares about whether the defendant gets convicted, but because he doesn't want the case coming back to him for a *retrial* after conviction. In other words, if the defendant forfeited his right to an attorney, then went to trial and lost, he may later allege that the trial judge didn't adequately inform him of his constitutional right to counsel. In that case, the conviction might be vacated and the case could be remanded (in other words, sent back) for a second trial, this time with an attorney. No trial judge wants this extra work, and most realize that it is better to spend fifteen minutes on "prevention" (questioning the defendant before trial) than it is to spend several days on a "cure" (conducting a second trial).

Let us assume that the judge is convinced that the defendant fully understands the right to, and importance of, a lawyer, and further that the defendant truly wishes to waive that right. The judge may then inquire about the defendant's competency for self-representation. This is not the same as competency to stand trial. Rather, competence for self-representation is a tougher test, and may require that the defendant be able to read and write English and have sufficient verbal skills to be able to conduct his own trial. It is quite possible that a defendant who is competent to stand trial *with* an attorney will *not* be considered competent to proceed to trial *without* an attorney. Not all states require this additional competence test, but some do in order to ensure that the defendant's right to *waive* counsel *and* his right *to* counsel are both adequately protected.[6]

Finally, even if the defendant satisfies this litany of inquiries—that is, he is competent to stand trial, fully understands the right to counsel and wishes to waive the right, and is competent to represent himself—the judge may still appoint a "stand-by counsel." In other words, the judge may appoint an attorney to stand by in the event that the defendant needs assistance in some way during the course of the trial. This stand-by counsel, however, technically serves the judge, not the defendant, and as long as the defendant is allowed to steer the course of his own defense, the stand-by counsel will not be deemed to have intruded upon the defendant's constitutional right to represent himself.[7]

In sum, if a person is accused of a crime but is mentally competent, capable of understanding the right to an attorney and the importance of an attorney, literate enough to read and write English, and able to verbally communicate fairly well, he will probably be allowed to represent himself at trial.

First Kill All the Lawyers

Chapter 30
Are public defenders "real lawyers"?

Yes. Public defenders are real lawyers who have been admitted to the bar and are licensed to practice in their jurisdiction. In fact, most public defenders are highly dedicated attorneys, and many are outstanding legal practitioners.

You wouldn't know it, though, by our popular culture. We've all seen a movie or television show that depicts the public defender as an inept attorney, overwhelmed by his role in the justice system and under-serving his clients. For example, in the movie *Wild Things*,[1] the private defense attorney, played by Bill Murray, reassures his client, played by Matt Dillon, that the good news is "you got a real attorney . . . instead of a public defender."[2] This depiction, although humorous, contributes to the widespread belief that public defenders aren't real lawyers, or if they are, they are not particularly effective ones.

Let us begin by explaining exactly who and what public defenders are. Public defenders are licensed attorneys who are employed by a state or the federal government to defend indigent citizens who are accused of crimes.[3] One part of every citizen's constitutional rights is that if she cannot afford an attorney, one will be appointed at government expense.[4] The public defenders are the attorneys who represent citizens who are accused of crimes but who are unable to pay for a private attorney.

So why do the stereotypes about public defenders persist? Probably the biggest reason is workload. The workload of some public defenders can be staggering. Often these attorneys must, through no choice of their own, represent two, three, or even four times the number of clients represented by an attorney in private practice. This obviously limits the amount of time and attention that a public defender is able to give to each individual client. As a result, a client may think that the public defender does not care about her case.

For example, given the great number of clients, trials, motions, and other court hearings, a public defender may not be able to return every client phone call, particularly when the client calls multiple times per week. Or, the public defender may never return phone calls from a client's family members or friends, as these people are not clients and are not directly affected by the case. But while the level of personal attention to clients may be decreased, the quality of the actual legal representation may be as good, or better, than that of many private defense attorneys. Nevertheless, there are limits. When an individual public defender's workload is heavy enough, it certainly can prevent him from rendering effective representation for clients.[5] In some states, public defenders have even taken legal action, arguing that they cannot render constitutionally effective representation when they are forced to represent many hundreds, and sometimes even thousands, of clients each year.[6]

The staggering workload is certainly a crucial element that affects the perceived quality—and in some cases, the actual quality—of a public defender's work, but there are also additional difficulties that public defenders face. Some studies have suggested that public defenders do not always obtain the same results for their clients as private defense attorneys do for theirs.[7] One reason for this may be that defending indigent clients poses numerous obstacles that often do not affect the private defense lawyer.

The citizens represented by public defenders are usually the truly indigent; even many people who are poor—that is, people whose income puts them below the poverty line—still will not qualify for representation by a public defender in some states. Therefore, when a public defender is assigned to a case, the client sometimes has limited education, lacks a supportive family system, is almost certainly unemployed, and at times is plagued by a history of contacts with law enforcement, which may actually stem from the client's socioeconomic status. It is therefore likely that—in the eyes of the arresting officers, the district attorney's office, and, ultimately, the court—this client already has a number of strikes against him. It is very probable that these factors, and not the attorneys' skill level, account for any difference in the actual outcome of cases between the clients of public defenders and the clients of private attorneys.

Additionally, many of the public defender's clients will be held in custody throughout the life of their case.[8] Obviously, when clients are indigent it is difficult for them to post bail after they have been accused of a crime. When they cannot post bail, they must remain in custody until, at the very least, their criminal case is concluded. This poses additional difficulties in representation. For example, instead of consulting with clients at a convenient time in the public defender's office—where legal books, a computer, and a phone are easily accessible—the public defender will have to go to the client's place of incarceration. This may involve significant travel time, and likely will mean that the time the attorney and the client spend together is limited. Conversely, in the case of very minor allegations, some defendants may be released on their own recognizance; many of these clients, however, may be transient, lacking a permanent home. This transience makes regular communication and good representation even more difficult.

Hence, the client who qualifies for representation by a public defender is often already "behind the eight ball," so to speak. Additionally, this client may garner less respect in the eyes of the police, the district attorney's office, and the court. This, of course may not be right, but it is often true, just the same. When the public defender comes on board to represent the client, he inherits all of this legal baggage, which makes the task of mounting a defense and obtaining a good outcome that much more difficult.

One truth about public defenders that deserves recognition is that these attorneys are much more likely to be skilled and experienced at trial than most general-practice private attorneys, whose work rarely takes them into that arena. Another truth about public defenders is that most demonstrate an incredible level of dedication to their clients and their cases. In fact, many who could easily have obtained higher-paying jobs will stay with the public defender's office—despite the low pay, heavy workload, increased obstacles, and unfair stereotypes—because they love and believe in the Constitution and in their work.

Last but certainly not least, there is another interesting fact about public defender representation that most people, including clients, don't know. Because most public defender offices, as a whole, have such a massive caseload, they will often farm out cases to *private* attorneys who will represent the clients at a reduced fee, to be paid by the public defender's office to the private attorney.[9] Consequently, and ironically, an attorney who a client *thinks* is a public defender—and therefore in the client's mind is not a "real lawyer"—may actually be a *private* attorney who has merely taken a case from the public defender's office to supplement his private practice.

Chapter 31
If you can't afford a lawyer, will the court appoint one for you?

Yes, but not as often as you may think, and possibly with strings attached.

In the United States Supreme Court case of *Gideon v. Wainwright*, the Court held that any person accused of a crime, "who is too poor to hire a lawyer, cannot be assured a fair trial unless counsel is provided for him. This seems to us to be an obvious truth. . . . The right of one charged with crime to counsel may not be deemed fundamental and essential to fair trials in some countries, but it is in ours."[1]

As we saw in the previous chapter, much of the indigent defense work in our country is handled by our various state public defender offices. However, as we also saw, it is often very difficult to qualify for public defender representation. If a defendant is denied representation, that leaves a court-appointed attorney as another means of fulfilling the *Gideon* mandate.

A court-appointed attorney is a lawyer assigned by the court to represent a defendant at little or no cost to the defendant. Sometimes, all of the costs and fees for this service will be waived, and other times, all or part of the costs and fees will be imposed on the defendant. In any case, a court-appointed attorney is both a necessity and usually a great value for a defendant, especially when compared to the cost of hiring private counsel. However, a defendant's financial situation must be fairly dire in order to become eligible for this court-appointed service.

The issue the court considers when determining a defendant's eligibility for a court-appointed attorney is the standard of "indigency," which is broadly defined in the legal system as "lack of ability to pay."[2] However, the court uses a number of factors to determine indigency, and many poor defendants are denied court-appointed attorneys because of the extremely strict guidelines by which indigency is often determined. Although the standards of indigency vary from state to state, and even from city to city, in many cases simply being poor—even living below the poverty level—may not qualify a defendant for a court-appointed attorney.

Consider the following example. Suppose that Barry and his landlord were going through a bitter dispute over their rental agreement. Then, in a particularly heated moment, Barry stormed off and drove his car erratically until he was pulled over by the police. To Barry's surprise, he was then charged criminally with reckless driving and was summoned to an initial court appearance, where the formal charges against him were presented for the first time. At this initial appearance, the judge or commissioner asked Barry if an attorney was representing him. Barry answered no. Not only did he not have the time or opportunity to contact a private attorney, but he didn't have the money to pay for one. In fact, he was already struggling financially after layoffs at his company. While Barry was lucky enough to find new employment, it was only for a minimum-wage job with part-time hours. Barry was already behind on his rent, and some of his outstanding bills had already gone to a collection agency.

It seems obvious that, under these circumstances, Barry needed only to *ask* for a court-appointed attorney, and he would *receive* one, right? Not necessarily. In many cases, to determine whether someone is truly indigent, and therefore qualifies for a court-appointed attorney, the court will consider the person's available assets as well as several other factors, perhaps including the following:

1) the receipt of certain public assistance payments, 2) income, after taxes, which does not exceed 125% of the current Federal Poverty Guideline, or 3) that a person cannot pay required fees or costs without depriving themselves or those who are dependent on them of the necessities of life, including food, shelter and clothing.[3]

However, these factors may vary dramatically from state to state and county to county. Further, it is important to remember that while determining indigency is very objective and mathematical, deciding on the initial indigency factors, and how much weight to give each of them, is very subjective. "Each state (or even county) makes its own rules as to who qualifies for a free lawyer."[4]

As we return to the example of our newly charged, and now-criminal-defendant Barry, the court required him to fill out financial paperwork to determine his financial standing. Because Barry earned a few hundred dollars each month, and because he had some assets such as a car, the court determined (to Barry's surprise) that he did not qualify for a court-appointed attorney. Barry had the right to then ask the court to grant him "partial indigency," in which the court would recognize that Barry, although not indigent, would be unable to pay the entire cost of a private attorney. If Barry qualified for partial indigency, he would have received the services of a court-appointed attorney but would have been required to pay for some of the costs of representation.[5]

As Barry's example shows, being underemployed, or even unemployed and receiving unemployment benefits, will count against an individual when determining indigency. Although it is obvious to most of us that a take-home pay of a few hundred dollars each month is not enough to pay for rent, groceries, bills, and transportation expenses, the standards that many courts use to determine indigency haven't changed for years or even decades. For example, in the 1970s a few hundred dollars in take-home pay might have covered routine living expenses, with some left over to pay a private lawyer. Today, however, a few hundred dollars is a drop in the bucket. Unfortunately, many of the old indigency thresholds have not been adjusted over time. As a result, a significant number of citizens living at *today's* poverty level may fail to qualify as indigent, and therefore may not qualify for a court-appointed attorney, at least not without significant cost to themselves.

However, there may be other, nonfinancial issues taken into account when determining indigency. For example, the gravity of the criminal charge may factor into the court's decision, and "a judge may recognize that a wage-earner can afford the cost of representation for a minor crime, but not for one involving a complicated and lengthy trial."[6] Additionally, the constitutionally guaranteed lawyer afforded to citizens by *Gideon v. Wainwright* applies only to some types of court cases:

> [Y]ou are entitled to an attorney if, on the charges you are being accused of, you face a period of incarceration. . . . If you are being prosecuted for a petty crime, however, in some instances you are not entitled to an attorney.[7]

Further, "[o]nly in criminal cases are you guaranteed a right to an attorney paid for by the state. In the civil courts, you must hire your own attorney."[8] Defendants in civil court matters—such as property disputes, contract disputes, divorces, and child custody matters, for example—do not qualify for court-appointed attorneys, at least not under *Gideon*. To return to our example, then, even if the court had declared Barry indigent and appointed him an attorney for his criminal reckless driving charge, Barry would *not* have been able to get a court-appointed attorney for his ongoing dispute with his landlord.[9]

But going back to the criminal reckless driving case, what if Barry *had* qualified as indigent, and the court appointed a lawyer for him, but Barry and the court-appointed lawyer didn't get along or see eye-to-eye on the case? When a defendant has money and privately retains a lawyer, it is usually fairly easy to fire the lawyer and hire a new one. But Barry, an indigent defendant, cannot simply fire the court-appointed lawyer in order to get a new one who would be better suited to his particular needs, or perhaps with whom he could better communicate.

While Barry might certainly *ask* the court for a different court-appointed attorney, the court could certainly deny such a request.[10] Generally, there would have to be good reason, and the attorney would likely have to agree with the request. Also, Barry should not fire his court-appointed attorney until he is sure that the court will approve his request for a new attorney. Otherwise, the court might interpret Barry's unsanctioned firing of his court-appointed attorney to mean that he no longer needed or wanted the services of *any* court-appointed attorney. In that case, Barry would have to either pay for a private attorney or represent himself.[11]

As a final point, anyone who is charged with a crime, no matter how minor it may seem, should always hire an attorney or request a court-appointed attorney. Unfortunately, there are many citizens who wrongly believe that a "misdemeanor charge" can't really hurt them, even if they are convicted. In many cases, these defendants will go through the criminal process by themselves, or worse yet, plead guilty thinking that it will "get the case over with" faster.[12] The reality, however, is that the effects of a criminal conviction, even for a misdemeanor, can be immediate, can linger for years, and can even linger for a lifetime.

An attorney trained in criminal law can do many things for a defendant, even when the defendant is accused of seemingly minor charges. First, an attorney can be beneficial both in suppressing the state's evidence as well as putting up a substantive defense at trial. Second, even if there is going to be a plea, an attorney can still negotiate favorable terms for the defendant and can also explain the consequences of a conviction. For example, even a misdemeanor conviction, depending on the specific crime, can lead to very harsh, long-term consequences, including: loss of child custody; lost employment opportunities; suspension of a driver's license; eviction from one's place of residence; disqualification from federal financial aid and other programs; and the permanent loss of the right to possess a firearm, to name only a few.[13]

Contract Law
A Deal Is a Deal

Chapter 32
Do contracts have to be in writing to be enforceable?

No. As a general rule, a contract does *not* have to be in writing, and an oral contract can be just as enforceable as a written one.

Many people confuse a contract with the piece of paper it's written on, and when there is no piece of paper they assume that there is no contract. In many cases, however, this assumption is false. Of course, from a practical standpoint, it helps to have things in writing in order to avoid disputes over the precise *terms* of the contract. But as far as the issue of whether a contract is legally *enforceable*, the general rule is that a written agreement is *not* required.[1]

First, what is a contract? Broadly speaking, a contract is defined as a promise or promises that are enforceable under the law.[2] Not all promises, however, are enforceable. In order for a promise to rise to the level of a contract, or an *enforceable* promise, there must be an offer and acceptance,[3] and an exchange of "consideration,"[4] also known as something of value.

Consider this simple example: Your aunt is packing up her belongings to move to a new home. During the moving process, she discovers an old painting that you've always liked. She tells you, "I'm going to have that painting framed and I promise to give it to you, would you like that?" You accept this nice gesture, but when the time comes to turn over the painting, your aunt changes her mind. Is her promise to you enforceable? No, at least not under contract theory. Why? Because it's just a promise standing all by itself and is therefore not a contract. Sure, there's an offer ("would you like the painting?") and an acceptance ("yes, thank you!"), but there is no exchange of *consideration*. In other words, you didn't give anything, or promise to do anything, in return for your aunt's promise to give you the painting.

Now, let's modify our example a bit. Suppose your aunt had said, "I'll get this painting framed and will sell it to you for three hundred dollars if you want to buy it." Because you love the painting, you reply, "Yes, I'll buy it. Let me know when it's framed and I'll pick it up and pay you." Is your aunt's promise to you enforceable? Yes, and so is your promise to her. Why? Because the two of you just entered into a contract. There is now an offer ("I'll sell you the framed painting for three hundred dollars"), an acceptance ("Yes, I'll buy it"), and the exchange of consideration. What's the consideration? Here, it's the exchange of promises—the promise to deliver the painting in exchange for the promise to pay money—which are both things of value and qualify as consideration. There are other ways to exchange consideration as well. Instead of *promising* to pay three hundred dollars, you could have actually *paid* the three hundred dollars on the spot. Either way, there is an exchange of consideration and, therefore, a binding contract.

As this example shows, many contracts are incredibly simple and straightforward, and we often enter into them without much thought or planning. On the other end of the spectrum, however, some contracts are mind-bogglingly complex. For example, when one corporation takes over or buys another corporation, the deal they strike is, in fact, a contract. This type of contract, however, will be in writing and could be hundreds of pages long. It could also involve the payment of millions or even billions of dollars in exchange for highly complicated, and very important, promises. And, unlike your purchase of the painting from your aunt, when corporate merger deals go bad, lawsuits *will* follow.

Finally, although the general rule is that a contract does *not* have to be in writing in order to be enforceable, some *do* have to be in writing. The corporate merger or takeover, discussed above, is one such example. Some other examples include contracts for the sale of land, contracts for the sale of goods over a certain dollar amount set by statute, and contracts that, by their terms, cannot be fully performed within one year.[5] There are other examples, to be sure, and the rules can certainly vary by state. As a result, anyone with a contract dispute, or anyone planning to enter into a contract of any significance, should consult with a licensed attorney in her state in order to sort through the legal thicket known as contract law.

Chapter 33
Will a contract be enforceable *because* it is in writing?

Not always.

As we saw in the previous chapter, some contracts *do* have to be in writing to be enforceable. However, while being in writing is sometimes a *necessary* condition for the enforcement of a contract, it is not, in and of itself, a *sufficient* condition. In other words, not all contracts will be enforceable *just because* they are in writing. In fact, there are many types of written contracts that are either unenforceable at the outset, or become unenforceable at some point after they are drawn up. In this chapter we'll discuss three such types, of many.

The first type is where the subject matter of the contract is, itself, illegal or against public policy.[1] In these cases, the written contract could be in perfect form, but it may still be unenforceable in whole or in part. There are numerous examples of contracts that are illegal or against public policy. For example, if I promise to deliver an ounce of cocaine to you, and you agree to pay me the street value upon delivery, that would be an illegal contract. Consequently, even if one of us blatantly breached the contract, the other could not sue in court. Since this contract was illegal from the outset and both of us knew it (or should have known it), it therefore is void (and probably even criminal in nature).

This cocaine deal is an obvious example of an illegal contract. Sometimes, however, the illegal nature of a contract isn't always clear, at least not right away. For example, if I agree to lease a commercial building to you so that you can run your manufacturing company, and we later learn that the property was not zoned for that type of activity, then I may not be able to enforce the contract against you. Why? Because the purpose of the contract would be in violation of the zoning laws and would therefore be illegal.[2] However, we may still have rights and obligations under the agreement. If, for example, you had paid me for the first month's rent, you may well be entitled to receive a refund of that amount, depending on the other facts surrounding our contract.

Whether the subject matter of a contract is illegal or against public policy obviously depends upon the law and the public policy in a given jurisdiction. What might be a legal and enforceable contract in one part of the country could well be *illegal* and *unenforceable* in another. Further, the rights of the parties to an illegal contract will also vary dramatically based on the particular facts of the case and the relevant law. However, some disturbing examples of illegal contracts include contracts for the sale of babies or bodily organs, contracts for hit men to commit murder, contracts for sexual favors (at least in most parts of the country), contracts for political or judicial favors from public officials, and contracts for the sale of United States Senate seats.[3]

The second type of unenforceable contract, even if in writing, is where there is some type of fraud involved in the making of the contract.[4] In these cases, the defrauded party might be able to avoid (or get out of) the contract or recover damages through contract law principles or other legal theories.

There are as many ways to commit fraud as there are individuals willing to commit it. For example, suppose that I'm an art dealer and I enter into a contract to sell you a valuable piece of artwork, which I represent as having been painted by Mr. Famous Artist. Our contract is put into writing, and the sale price is $15,000. Normally, this contract would be enforceable; not only did we set forth our agreement in writing, but there's nothing at all illegal about selling artwork in our jurisdiction. However, unbeknownst to you at the time you signed the contract, I intentionally misled you when I told you that the artwork was painted by Mr. Famous Artist. It turns out that it was actually painted by Mr. *Infamous* Artist, and isn't worth the canvas it's painted on.

In this case, if we assume you haven't yet paid the $15,000, you may well be able to avoid the contract, even though it was in writing. Conversely, assuming you *have* paid the $15,000 and our transaction was completed, you may still have other options available to you under contract doctrine or other legal theories. In other words, all is not lost, and you may still be able to get a refund of your money by filing a civil lawsuit.

The third type of unenforceable contract, even if in writing, is where the goal of the contract was perfectly legitimate at the time the contract was signed but has subsequently become impossible to fulfill.[5] In these cases, the contract may also be unenforceable, in whole or in part, and one or both parties may have legal rights against the other.

For example, suppose that I contract with you to rent you a house that I own. We agree on the lease terms and put our contract in writing, which calls for you to move into the house on the first of next month. Unfortunately, when you show up with your U-Haul packed full of furniture, you are shocked to see that the house has burned to the ground.

In this case, we had a written contract with a perfectly legitimate purpose to begin with. Then, unfortunately, due to factors outside of our control, the subject matter of our contract—the house—was destroyed. In this case, it is impossible to fulfill the contract, and therefore it will be unenforceable. Again, however, both of us may have legal rights in this case, but neither of us can enforce a rental contract for a property that no longer exists.

These are just three examples of contracts that may be unenforceable, even when they are in writing. Other reasons for contracts being unenforceable also exist. As a later chapter will illustrate, there may be nearly as many ways *out of* contracts as there are *types of* contracts.

Chapter 34
Can promises be enforced, even if they're not enforceable as contracts?

Yes, sometimes.

As we saw in the first of our chapters on contracts, an enforceable contract consists of a promise. However, we also learned that *more* than just a promise is necessary to create an enforceable contract. There also has to be consideration, which is often in the form of an *exchange* of promises. For example, if the furniture store promises to deliver a new couch to my home, and I promise to pay them the agreed-upon price when they deliver it, then we may very well have a binding contract, assuming that all of the other elements are present.

But what happens if, for example, I promise my next-door neighbor that I will cut his grass this Saturday when I'm out cutting my own lawn? Or what if I promise to pay my daughter's college tuition for a semester because she earned an A in Physics? Or if I promise to pay the first three months' payments on my son's car loan if he decides to buy a new car? Those promises aren't contracts, because there is no exchange of consideration. In other words, my neighbor isn't promising to pay me or do anything for me in return for my cutting his grass. My daughter, although she did well in Physics in the past, isn't promising to do anything in the future in exchange for me paying her college tuition bill for a semester. And my son isn't promising to do anything for me in exchange for my paying his first three months of car payments.

So then the question becomes: even if a promise isn't part of a binding contract, can it still be enforceable, and if so, under what theory? The answer is yes, it can be, and the theory behind it is called "promissory estoppel." In order to enforce a promise under this theory, however, there still has to be more than a mere promise. Although the precise formulation will vary from state to state, under this theory of promissory estoppel: (1) there has to be a definite promise; (2) the person making the promise (the promisor) should reasonably expect that the other person (the promisee) will rely on the promise; (3) the promisee has to *actually* rely to his detriment on the promise; (4) the reliance has to be reasonable; and (5) enforcing the promise is necessary in order to avoid injustice.[1]

So what does this mean for our previous, hypothetical examples? Would the promisee, or the person to whom I made the promise, in each of these examples be able to legally enforce my promise? Let's start with the next-door neighbor. What if, when I cut my own lawn on Saturday, I renege on my promise and refuse to cut his lawn? Well, there was a fairly definite and clear promise; that is, there was nothing at all vague about what I promised to do. But did my neighbor really *rely* on my promise to his detriment? Probably not. And would it be unjust if the promise went unenforced? Again, probably not. The only downside for my neighbor is that now he has to cut his own lawn, which is something he'd have to do anyway. So this promise certainly isn't enforceable as a contractual promise, and probably isn't enforceable under the theory of promissory estoppel either.

How about my daughter? What if I renege on my promise to pay her college tuition for a semester? Aside from my being a disappointing father, would she be able to enforce my promise? There was a very specific and definite promise. But did she rely on the promise to her detriment, and if so, was her reliance reasonable? For example, did my daughter enroll in school *because of* my promise? If yes, then that would probably be reliance, and reasonable reliance at that. Or was she already in school and would have continued to go to school regardless of whether I made the promise? In that case, she didn't do anything because of my promise, and therefore reliance, reasonable or otherwise, was probably not a factor. But could she have relied on it in some other way? For example, did she quit her part-time job because she was counting on my tuition payment? Did she forgo signing up for student loans because of my promise? Depending on the answers to all of these questions, my daughter may certainly have a case for enforcing my promise under the theory of promissory estoppel.

Finally, what about my son, who goes out and buys an automobile after I promised to make the first three months' payments? Can he enforce my promise? It seems that this may be the strongest case yet for enforcement. There is a definite and specific promise; it's reasonable for me to expect that, based on my promise, my son will actually buy the car; and it would probably be unjust for me to saddle him with the first three payments after I promised that I would make them. This case may come down to whether my son's reliance was reasonable. For example, if he bought a two-year-old Honda Civic, that might very well be reasonable reliance. In that case, the promise may very well be enforceable. However, if he instead went out and bought a brand-new Ferrari, something that neither one of us could afford, then his reliance could very well be unreasonable, and the promise would not be enforceable.

The lesson here, for both sides, is to proceed with caution. If you're the one making the promise, don't promise anything you won't deliver. If you're the one receiving the promise, don't take every promise so seriously.

Chapter 35
Can a minor (under eighteen years old) enter into a contract?

Yes. Minors can, and do, enter into contracts all the time.

For example, you may recall the episode of the popular television series *The Simpsons*, where ten-year-old Bart Simpson signed a contract selling his soul for five dollars.[1] Bart *is* a minor, and the agreement to sell his soul for the five-dollar payment *is* a contract; after all, there is an offer, an acceptance, and the exchange of consideration.[2] However, metaphysical issues aside, the more pertinent question is whether Bart's contract is really *enforceable*.

As it turns out, certain groups of people do *not* have what is called "full capacity" to contract. Minors, or persons under eighteen years old, are one such group. They have only a "limited capacity" to contract.[3] What this means is that minors certainly *can* enter into contracts; and from a practical standpoint, their contracts usually work out just fine for everyone involved. Nevertheless, because of the limited capacity of minors, they have a special power when entering into contracts. Minors are able to legally "avoid," or get out of, their contracts after they've entered into them. The justification for this rule is, in theory, obvious: Because of their youth and inexperience, minors need additional protection under the law. So while Bart, a minor, *did* enter into a contract, the relevant point is that he could probably get out of it if he knew his rights. (Never mind, for our purposes, that the other contracting party, Milhouse, was also a minor.)

Let's move to a more realistic example. Assume that Joey, a sixteen-year-old minor, decides he wants to buy a car. He goes to the local Cars-R-Us dealership and finds a nice, shiny new sports car with a sticker price of $32,000. The salesman, having a slow month and eager to make a deal, sells the car to Joey for $30,000, and for no money down. Instead of money down, he signs Joey up for full financing through the dealership's finance department. There's even a special promotion: no payments for the first year.

Joey's purchase of the car clearly *is* a contract. Joey made an offer to buy the car and the salesman accepted. Specific promises were also exchanged: Joey promised to pay principal and interest payments beginning in one year, and the dealership promised to deliver the shiny new sports car. Joey signed the paperwork, and a few minutes later he rolled off the lot in his brand-new car. Everyone was happy about the deal.

One year later, however, when the first payment comes due, Joey starts to have second thoughts. Joey, now wiser, but still a minor at the ripe old age of seventeen, wishes he hadn't bought the car. Sure it was fun to drive, and it served its purpose for a year, but he really doesn't want to make those payments. He'll be headed off to college soon and he sure could think of better uses for the money. So Joey writes the dealership and tells the manager that, because he's a minor, he's not going to be making any payments! He's getting out of—or as the law calls it, "avoiding"—the contract.

Can Joey do this? You bet. If the car dealership were to sue him to make the payments under the contract, Joey would probably win. As a minor, "avoidance" is a defense, and this defense would likely prevail. The only thing Joey has to do is return the car, or what's left of it, regardless of how many miles he's put on it and regardless of whether or not it has been damaged. And if it has been stolen, then there's nothing left to return at all, and Joey can still avoid the contract and legally refuse to make payments.[4] Obviously, Cars-R-Us would be furious. After all, Joey drove the car for free for that whole year, hadn't yet made a single payment (because payments were deferred for a year), and put a lot of wear-and-tear on the car. The darned thing has probably depreciated by nearly half, and, according to the law, that's just too bad.

When a party deals with minors, that party takes on the risks of doing so. And for that reason, a knowledgeable party would be very cautious about entering into such a significant contract with a minor. Conversely, because many minors—and older teens in particular—have a tremendous amount of disposable income, it would be foolish for a business not to sell its products to them. The situation obviously requires a careful risk-reward analysis, taking into account what product is being sold and the likelihood of the minor avoiding the contract.

Now, if you're a minor who is planning a spending spree, or if you're a business owner and want to assess the real risks of dealing with minors, you need to see an attorney. Why? There are at least four reasons.

First, there are many exceptions to the general rule that a minor can avoid his contracts. For example, if the minor enters into a contract to purchase what are called "necessities," then the minor may *not* be able to later avoid the contract, or at least may have a limited ability to do so.[5] For example, if the minor buys very basic, non-frivolous food and clothing, those items would probably be considered necessities, and under those circumstances the law would give far more protection to the adult party and less protection to the minor party.

Second, there are many subtleties to this law. For example, sometimes the contract that the minor seeks to avoid *has yet to be performed.* This means that the parties each agreed to do something under the contract but haven't yet done it. On the other hand, sometimes the contract *has been fully performed* and is now a completed transaction. This means that both parties have already done everything they agreed to do under the contract. For example, if a minor goes to a rummage sale and makes an offer to buy an old lamp, and the offer is accepted, there is a contract. At that point, the parties have yet to perform their obligations under the contract. However, once the minor pays for the lamp, and the seller gives the lamp to the minor, the contract becomes a completed transaction. The category to which a particular contract belongs may have a substantial impact on the rights of the parties, from both a legal and a practical standpoint.[6]

Third, every state law is different and has its own general rule, subrules, and exceptions. For example, what counts as a necessity under California's law may be quite different from a necessity under Florida's law. As another example, if a minor misrepresents his age as being eighteen years or older, and then later seeks to avoid a contract that he entered into under this misrepresentation, some states may allow him to avoid the contract and some may not.[7]

Fourth, through the passage of time, or through certain other actions, the minor may actually bind himself to the contract. For example, if the minor waits too long and turns eighteen years old, it might be too late to avoid the contract.[8]

When it comes to minors and contracts, there's no way to know your rights or obligations without consulting an attorney who knows both your facts and the state's laws. And after your meeting with the attorney, if you're a minor, you can add an ironic twist to your attorney-client relationship: You can try to "avoid" the attorney-client contract by refusing to pay for the legal services just rendered.[9]

Chapter 36
Are disclaimers, or no-liability clauses, enforceable?

It depends.

Anyone who has ever bought a "service" of any kind has probably, at some point, come across a disclaimer or no-liability clause. In legal jargon, these are typically known as "exculpatory clauses" because they attempt to exculpate, or excuse, one of the parties from liability in the event someone gets hurt or property is damaged.

Exculpatory clauses have been used on the back of tickets for entry into sporting events, in contracts for medical or legal services, in contracts for gym memberships, and in releases required for skiing, swimming, skydiving, horseback riding, and a host of other activities. The reason these exculpatory clauses are used is that, sometimes, things go badly. For example, sometimes spectators at baseball games get beaned with foul balls or flying baseball bats. Sometimes doctors make mistakes and their patients get hurt. And sometimes people who go skiing, swimming, skydiving, and horseback riding get injured or even die. And when these bad things happen, the injured parties or their families may want to file a lawsuit to be compensated for the injury.

When these lawsuits are filed, the plaintiffs often try to get money by claiming that the defendant, the party who provided the services, was negligent. In other words, the plaintiff will claim that the defendant did not exercise reasonable care, thus leading to the injury. The defendant, however, could defend the lawsuit by arguing in court that she did, in fact, exercise reasonable care, and therefore the injury was not her fault. For example, if a want-to-be supermodel suffers injury from a plastic surgery procedure, he may file a lawsuit and argue to the jury that the doctor was negligent and therefore should pay him money. The doctor, however, could argue that she did everything right, followed all reasonable procedures, and took all reasonable precautions; therefore she wasn't negligent. Sometimes, the doctor could argue, bad things happen and it's no one's fault.

The problem with this, however, is that it costs a lot of money and time for the defendant and the defendant's insurance company. Therefore, potential defendants would like to prevent would-be plaintiffs from even filing their lawsuits in the first place. Therefore, a potential defendant may put an exculpatory clause into the contract that he or she enters into with the would-be plaintiff. Here's an example of such a clause, from an actual case, used by a fitness center in its membership contracts:

WAIVER RELEASE STATEMENT

I AGREE TO ASSUME ALL LIABILITY FOR MYSELF WITHOUT REGARD TO FAULT, WHILE AT THE FITNESS CENTER. I FURTHER AGREE TO HOLD HARMLESS THE FITNESS CENTER, OR ANY OF ITS EMPLOYEES FOR ANY CONDITIONS OR INJURY THAT MAY RESULT TO MYSELF WHILE AT THE FITNESS CENTER. I HAVE READ THE FORE-GOING AND UNDERSTAND ITS CONTENTS.[1]

The question, then, is this: If a person signs a contract with one of these exculpatory clauses in it, and then gets injured, can he still sue for negligence, or does the exculpatory clause prevent the lawsuit? Generally speaking, the law disfavors these types of clauses, because they allow a party (here, the fitness center) to be negligent and then escape all potential liability and responsibility for its negligence. Therefore, in order for one of these clauses to be valid and enforceable against would-be plaintiffs, it has to be well drafted and meet certain standards. In sum, then, the answer to the question depends on a number of different facts and circumstances.

One of the factors that courts will look at when deciding

whether the exculpatory clause is enforceable is whether it was clear and specific about the risks being assumed and the specific type of activities that give rise to those risks. For example, a clause may be very clear, warning baseball spectators that foul balls are frequently hit into the stands and could cause injury, including head injury, and therefore spectators should be alert for this at all times.[2] In this case, the warning is very clear about the specific type of injury (head trauma), as well as what gives rise to the injury (foul balls). This type of specificity and clarity is a big factor in favor of upholding the exculpatory clause, which would, of course, prevent a lawsuit from going forward.

On the other hand, an exculpatory clause may be very vague about the type of injury that could occur, as well as what could cause it. For example, the fitness center's exculpatory clause, cited above, simply refers to "any conditions or injury that may result," without specifying *what* those injuries might be or *how* they might occur.[3] That particular clause was held to be unenforceable and therefore did not prevent the plaintiff from suing for injuries sustained. The reason was that the fitness center was essentially being too broad and was trying to protect itself from everything that could possibly go wrong, without giving any notice to its members of the actual risks or which activities caused those risks.

Another factor that the courts will look at is whether the plaintiff was given fair notice of the exculpatory clause. If the clause was buried in fine print, or placed inconspicuously in the middle of a multipage document, for instance, that would weigh against its enforceability. On the other hand, if the clause stands out in some way—for example, if it is printed in large, colored, or bold font—then that would be a factor weighing in favor of its validity and enforceability.[4] The point here is that the more conspicuous the notice, or the more it stands out, the better the chance that the plaintiff actually knew about it before she signed the contract. And of course, if the plaintiff had noticed and knew about the clause, the argument is stronger that she should have to live by its terms, and therefore should be barred from suing the defendant.

Yet another factor that the courts may consider in deciding whether the clause is enforceable is the relative bargaining power of the parties. For example, if the service provider defendant had a take-it-or-leave-it attitude with regard to the contract and the exculpatory clause, then this suggests a gross imbalance in bargaining power and is a factor weighing against enforceability. On the other hand, if there was a give-and-take negotiation between the parties before signing the contract, then that suggests a more level playing field, in which case the plaintiff is more likely to be bound by the clause and its terms.[5] Often, this power disparity is correlated with the number of alternative service providers available to the plaintiff before entering into the contract with the particular defendant. For example, were there other fitness centers in the area from which to choose, or was the defendant's fitness center the only game in town? If there were other fitness centers, giving the plaintiff other options, then the exculpatory clause would more likely be enforceable.

Finally, perhaps the biggest factor is the nature of the service being provided. If the service is a necessity, such as basic medical services or legal services in defense of a criminal allegation, then public policy would probably dictate that the service provider may not use an exculpatory clause to limit his liability, no matter how specific or conspicuous the clause actually is.[6] On the other hand, activities such as skiing and skydiving are not necessary at all, and therefore exculpatory clauses are much more likely to be enforced, especially when they are clearly worded and disclaim liability only for very specific risks.

The bottom line, of course, is that you should carefully read every contract that you sign. However, even if you do sign an exculpatory clause and are later injured, it doesn't necessarily mean that you can't sue. So the lesson is that under such a circumstance, you should consult with your lawyer immediately.

Chapter 37
Are there legal ways to get out of an otherwise enforceable contract?

Yes, absolutely. If you look hard enough, there may be a way out of nearly any deal.

We've already seen, in previous chapters, how a party can get out of a contract on several different bases. Some of these bases depend on who the party is; for example, a minor who has special rights and wants to avoid, or get out of, a contract. Other bases depend on the facts and circumstances of the case; for example, where the subject or purpose of the contract has been destroyed or no longer exists, enforcement of the contract may not be possible. And yet others depend on the form of the contract; for example, some contracts must be in writing or they cannot be enforced.

But there are yet other ways to escape an otherwise valid and enforceable contract, or at least portions of the contract. One such way is to use the doctrine of *unconscionability*. This doctrine states that if a contract is so unfair that it is unconscionable, then it will not be enforced. The basis for this doctrine is that when two parties enter into a contract, one of them may have more bargaining power, or will be more sophisticated or educated, than the other. When such imbalance exists, and when the powerful and sophisticated party takes extreme advantage of the other party, the contract may, in some circumstances, be unconscionable and therefore unenforceable.

But what is an unconscionable contract? Typically, it can be thought of as a contract that is so unfair as to "affront the sense of decency."[1] As you may have guessed, however, this language is so vague that courts' interpretations of this doctrine are inconsistent and often irreconcilable, giving "the sensitive a feeling of lawlessness, the logician a feeling of irrationality and the average lawyer a feeling of confusion."[2]

In any case, the party wishing to escape the contract under this doctrine must affirmatively show that certain facts exist.[3] First, were the contract terms preposterously one-sided? The most common example of this is where the contract price is itself excessive relative to the true market value of the goods or services being provided. Other one-sided contract terms may include, for example, having the weaker party waive all rights and warranties under a sales contract, or agree to strictly limited damages that she may otherwise have in the event of a future lawsuit.

However, just because a contract is incredibly one-sided doesn't mean that the weaker of the parties can get out of his end of the bargain. The second factor that courts will look at is whether the weaker party knew of, and accepted, the one-sided terms to begin with. If yes, then the contract may be enforceable. However, if the one-sided terms were hidden in the small print, or were couched in confusing legalese, then the weaker party may not have been given fair and proper notice of the one-sided nature of the agreement. This, then, would be a factor in favor of a finding of unconscionability.

The third factor, and something that we've already alluded to, is the imbalance between the parties. Is one party a giant corporation with multiple attorneys representing it, while the other party is an uneducated and unsophisticated individual consumer? If so, and if the individual consumer has little choice but to accept the one-sided terms, this would weigh in favor of unconscionability. On the other hand, even if the contract were one-sided, it may not be unconscionable if the consumer had the ability to simply walk away and strike a better deal with a competing company across town. In other words, the choices and options available to consumers may also come into play.

The law of unconscionability often takes on different labels, is covered by numerous different laws, and often varies dramatically based on a given state's law. The law will also vary based on whether the item purchased was a good or a service, and whether there is an applicable federal law. In any case, a claim of unconscionability is one way, although not an easy way, to escape contractual liability.

Another way to escape a contract is through the doctrine of *frustration of purpose*. This doctrine may excuse a person from performing under a contract when the original purpose for entering into the contract has been frustrated.[4] (Although other factors must also be satisfied, we will limit our discussion to this single factor.)

For example, suppose that a tennis fan living in California decides to attend the US Open—one of the world's four "major" tennis tournaments—in New York. When making his plans, he enters into an agreement to rent a house right on the train-line about ten miles away from the city. The agreement specifically states that the tennis fan will pay a fixed sum, and in exchange may use the premises "for residential purposes for the first two weeks of September 2012 during the US Open tennis tournament."

But then, unexpectedly, due to a natural disaster in the New York area, the tournament is delayed by one month and will instead be played at a nearby facility indoors *during the month of October*. Can the tennis fan get out of his lease for the "first two weeks of September"? Quite possibly. After all, both parties knew that the sole reason for the lease was so that the tennis fan could see the US Open. But because the US Open was unexpectedly delayed, the purpose of the contract—that is, to provide housing during the time of the US Open tennis tournament—has been frustrated. Yes, it would still be possible to travel to New York, pay the rent, and live in the house for the first two weeks of September, but there would be no reason for the tennis fan to do so.

But the frustration of purpose doctrine has its limits.[5] Suppose the tennis fan is really a fan of a specific tennis player. What if that player had to pull out of the US Open at the last minute due to injury? Would the fan then be able to claim frustration of purpose? After all, if not for the chance to see his favorite player in person, the fan would probably be watching the tournament from his television set in California. Most likely, however, this would not be enough to get out of the lease. Why? Because to use the frustration of purpose doctrine, the purpose must be completely, or nearly completely, frustrated. Just because the fan's favorite player is injured isn't enough, as the fan can still come to the tournament and enjoy world-class tennis from other players on the tour.

The doctrines of unconscionability and frustration of purpose only touch the surface of the possible ways to escape contracts. Other doctrines, some of which are closely related, include undue influence, nondisclosure, unilateral and mutual mistake, and, perhaps most interestingly, plain breach of contract. That's right; sometimes the quickest and easiest way out of a contract is simply to breach it. Why? Putting aside the issue of whether purposely reneging on a deal is immoral or unethical, breaching may be the most economically sensible way to go.

In many cases, a lawsuit by the nonbreaching party may not be cost effective, and even further, there may not be any damages to pursue. (In many cases, in order to recover money in a lawsuit, the nonbreaching party has to have suffered some financial loss, or damages.) In other cases, there may in fact be damages, but they may be predetermined by the contract itself, a concept known as liquidated damages.[6] For example, if a residential cable subscriber breaches his contract with the cable company, he may have to pay damages of $150, an amount predetermined by his subscriber contract. In that case, the damages owed may be far less costly than sticking to the contract. Therefore, breaching the contract may actually make sense, at least in economic terms, though possibly not in moral or ethical terms. Of course, breaching a contract, or trying to use legal doctrines to escape a contract, should only be done after consulting a licensed attorney.

Family Law
Love and Marriage

Chapter 38
If you break up with your fiancé, can you keep the ring?

Maybe. The answer depends on your particular state's law, and it could even depend on the reason for the break-up.

Let's look at an example: Brad and Stephanie were positive that they were meant to be together. They and all of their friends just *knew* that they were a match made in heaven. And although they had only recently met, it wasn't long before Brad popped the question and asked Stephanie to marry him. Stephanie couldn't resist, and, much to everyone's delight, the couple was engaged to be married. Brad, who was doing quite well for himself financially, gave her a beautiful (and *very* expensive) diamond engagement ring that was equaled in brilliance only by the sparkle in Stephanie's eyes.

Before the wedding could even be planned, however, the relationship between Brad and Stephanie took an unexpected turn for the worse. Much to their surprise, each had initially been blinded by lust, rather than love, and neither was really the person the other had thought. As a result, they decided to cut their losses and call off the wedding, to the dismay of all their friends. And to make matters worse, their parting wasn't exactly amicable. For Brad, although Stephanie had lost her luster, the engagement ring he gave her had not. Therefore, he wanted it back. Stephanie, however, had different plans and wanted to keep the ring—or, more accurately, the proceeds from its sale—as a reminder of her whirlwind romance with Brad. When the two couldn't reach a resolution, Brad decided to sue her in state court for the return of the ring.

Now, this is a tough one. Matters of the heart can be problematic, and engagement rings even more so. As a New York court wisely recognized:

> The ring is employed in rites of courtship and marriage in many cultures, primitive and sophisticated; in widely dispersed regions of the earth; persisting through the centuries, in fact millennia. In our culture, the ring generally is placed on one of the fingers, in others it may be attached to other positions of the anatomy, at intermediate points from the top of the head to the tip of the toes. It is a universal symbol of deep seated sexual and social ramifications, a seminal area of research for behavioral scientists. *Is it any wonder that it presents such complicated problems for mere lawyers?*[1]

But, alas, there *is* an answer to the dispute between Brad and Stephanie. An engagement ring, at first glance, may look like a gift. Of course, we all know that, once given, a gift does *not* have to be returned. However, the predominant legal view is that an engagement ring is a special kind of gift known as a "conditional gift" or a "provisional gift," and there are special rules that go with it.[2] Not to be outdone by the eloquent New York court, a Pennsylvania court explained it this way:

> A gift given by a man to a woman on condition that she embark on the sea of matrimony with him is not different from a gift based on the condition that the [woman] sail on any other sea. If, after receiving the provisional gift, the [woman] refuses to leave the harbor,—if the anchor of contractual performance sticks in the sands of irresolution and procrastination—the gift must be restored to the donor.[3]

In other words, Brad gave Stephanie the ring with the expectation that the two would marry. The act of marriage is known as the "condition" or "provision" that must be fulfilled. When their marriage fell through—or, more eloquently stated, when it got stuck "in the sands of irresolution and procrastination"—the condition was *not* fulfilled, and Stephanie therefore must return the ring.

But wait, what if Brad was a real cad? What if he cheated on

Stephanie, and when Stephanie confronted him about it, it was *Brad* who actually broke off the engagement and broke Stephanie's heart in the process. That's pretty terrible behavior. Shouldn't Stephanie be allowed to keep the ring, or at least sell it in order to get something for her suffering? That depends on the law of the ex-couple's state of residence. Some states will simply say that it doesn't matter who broke up with whom, or why they did so. The ring was gifted on the condition of marriage, and for whatever reason the condition (marriage) didn't happen. Consequently, the ring must be returned.[4]

The reasoning is that, if the opposite were the case, and courts had to determine which of the parties was the wrongdoer, such a system would "simply condone this same type of [wrongdoing] in yet another form. The result would be to encourage every disappointed donee to resist the return of engagement gifts by blaming the donor for the break-up of the contemplated marriage, *thereby promoting dramatic courtroom accusations and counter-accusations of fault.*"[5]

Nevertheless, in most states, Brad would *only* win his lawsuit to recover the ring if he was not the one at fault. In other words, in order to win his lawsuit against Stephanie for the ring, Brad would have to prove to the court that he did not unjustifiably call off the wedding.[6] Inevitably, trials on this issue will have to explore the "murky depths of contradictory, acrimonious, and largely irrelevant testimony by disappointed couples, their relatives and friends."[7] And by the time that's done, Brad may find that he's spent more in legal fees and court costs than the ring was worth in the first place.

Chapter 39
In a divorce, does the mother have an advantage over the father for child custody?

No, at least not directly.

The mere fact that one parent is a woman and is the child's mother should not, in and of itself, matter one bit in determining child custody during a divorce. In fact, although the statutes governing divorce and child custody vary by state, the law will often explicitly instruct that, when making a decision on child custody, "the court may *not* prefer one parent . . . over the other on the basis of the *sex* or race of the parent . . ."[1]

So how, then, do courts make custody determinations? The short answer is that courts will decide based on the "best interest of the child."[2] However, there is a little more structure to it than that. But we first need to determine what type of custody we're talking about. When there is a divorce, and the couple has a child, the court must decide both *legal* and *physical* custody for the child. *Legal* custody refers to a parent's right to make legal decisions for the child, such as where the child will go to school, or what religion, if any, the child will be exposed to. *Physical* custody refers to where and with whom the child will reside.

With regard to legal custody, the law can be relatively straightforward. Many laws will presume that *joint* legal custody—that is, both parents sharing in the decision making—is in the best interest of the child.[3] Further, this legal presumption means that, unless there is strong evidence to the contrary to rebut the presumption, the court must order that the legal custody is joint, and therefore shared by both parents. (This essentially ensures that, whenever there are children involved, there can never be a completely clean and total break between the parties in a divorce.)

So how can the presumption be rebutted? The statute will probably provide for specific ways that one of the parties may do that.[4] The presumption might be rebutted, and only one parent will be awarded sole legal custody, if both parents agree that it is best and if the court also believes that sole legal custody would be in the best interest of the child. Or, the presumption might be rebutted if one parent requests sole legal custody and is able to show that the other parent was physically abusive during the marriage, or would somehow be unable to carry out normal parental duties such as making common legal decisions that a parent must make throughout a child's life. Barring an unusual situation like that, however, if a state law subscribes to the presumption of joint legal custody, then both parents will be sharing legal custody, and consequently will be sharing the decision making until their child becomes an adult.

With regard to physical custody, while the courts may try to give some amount or level of custody to each parent, it normally will not be shared equally, as it is in the case of legal custody. Furthermore, while "the court may *not* prefer one parent . . . over the other on the basis of the *sex* or race of the parent,"[5] it turns out that many of the factors that the court must consider may naturally favor the mother. This is not due to the fact that the mother is a woman, but rather due to the parental role that a mother typically plays in our society. Here, then, are some factors that courts may be required to consider when deciding who gets physical custody of the child, and how much physical custody that party gets:

1. Whether the parents jointly agree on a physical custody allocation plan. (For example, perhaps the mother and father will jointly agree that, due to the father's work schedule, the mother should have the child on the weekdays, and the father should have the child on the weekends.)
2. The child's wishes as to where he or she would like to reside.
3. The relative amount of time spent with each parent *before* the divorce, and the reasonable life changes a parent is willing to make *after* the divorce to allow for more time with the child.

4. The child's age and educational needs, as well as the child's need for stability and predictability.
5. The effect that other people in each parent's household may have on the child's physical or emotional well-being. (For example, if one parent decides to reside with a relative who has a physical or psychological disorder, this could be a factor in determining the best interests of the child.)
6. Whether one parent has a history of domestic abuse, child abuse, or sexual abuse, or is now dating or residing with someone who has criminal convictions for such acts.
7. Any known drug or alcohol use by the parents.
8. The recommendations of professionals involved in the case.[6]

These are just a handful of the factors that may be considered by a court in determining physical custody. In many cases, some or most of these factors may naturally favor the mother. Additionally, because there are so many factors, and because the court can weigh some of them more heavily than others, determining the physical custody plan that is in the best interest of the child is highly subjective. The vagueness of this determination, and the flexibility afforded in reaching it, certainly gives a judge the opportunity to favor the mother simply because she is a woman, despite the letter of the law.

Chapter 40
In a divorce, can a "pre-nup" protect your assets from your ex-spouse?

Yes, probably to some extent, but not entirely.

Hollywood, the media, and the American public seem to really love ugly divorce battles. Whether it's Donald and Ivana Trump, Alec Baldwin and Kim Basinger, or movies along the lines of *The War of the Roses*, the more bitter the battle, the more it captivates us. And of course, with many divorces come prenuptial agreements, also known as "pre-nups" for short. Either the parties to a divorce have one and are fighting over it, or one or both of the parties wished they had one. In either case, the pre-nup is as much a part of family law as love and marriage.

First, what exactly is a pre-nup? In simple terms, it's a written agreement, signed by the parties before marriage, which spells out precisely how the parties' assets are to be divided between them in the event of a divorce. Pre-nups have long been hated by many (including the poorer of the two spouses) because they presume the one thing—a divorce—that should be farthest from a soon-to-be-married couple's minds. On the other hand, rich spouses, lawyers, and the less-romantic among us have praised them as an excellent way to protect assets and family fortunes should the marriage fail.[1]

But how effective are pre-nups? Can the rich heiress, for example, really make her young boy-toy, soon-to-be husband sign one? And if he does sign it, will it really allow her to keep all of her assets while leaving her ex-husband with nothing? When the shoe is on the other foot, can the old, gray-haired billionaire really make his young supermodel wife sign one? And if she does sign it, can he dump her at will for next year's hot supermodel, leaving her without a dime to her name?

Probably not. Despite the image that Hollywood may portray, the law is quite a different story. Like many areas of law, the law on pre-nups varies from state to state. Generally, however, in order for a pre-nup to be enforceable, it must be equitable, or fair. In determining whether the pre-nup is fair, and therefore enforceable, the court can look to a number of more specific things, including: (1) whether each spouse fully disclosed his or her assets to the other spouse prior to signing the agreement; (2) whether each spouse freely entered into the pre-nup; and (3) whether the asset distribution was fair when signed, and is fair now, upon divorce.[2]

Let's take an example to try and make sense of this. Suppose that Mr. Rich Husband is divorcing Mrs. Model Wife. Husband wants to enforce the pre-nup that Wife signed before their marriage. The pre-nup limits Wife to only $500,000 of the total assets, and she believes this is unfair and wants more. (This may at first glance seem inappropriately greedy on Wife's part, but don't judge Wife just yet. Read on.)

The first issue, according to our legal standard that we've adopted above, is whether there was full disclosure by Husband at the time the pre-nup was signed. Was Husband honest and upfront about his assets? Or did he lie and hide some? For example, when negotiating the pre-nup, if Husband told Wife he was worth $2 million, then getting $500,000 (or 25 percent of the money) that otherwise wouldn't be hers may have seemed quite reasonable from Wife's standpoint. But what if it turned out that Husband lied? What if he were actually worth $2 *billion* at the time they signed the pre-nup? Not only would that be deceitful, but the $500,000 would suddenly become a pathetic fraction of the true value of the total assets. If he had lied, that would be a pretty big strike against Husband in his battle to have the pre-nup enforced.

The second issue is whether Wife freely entered into the pre-nup. For example, if Wife had time to read the pre-nup, think about it, and hire a lawyer to review it for her if she wanted, then that would tend to indicate that she *did* enter into the agreement freely, by her own choice. On the other hand, if Husband sprung it on her the day before the wedding and told her that *his* lawyer said that she "had to sign it today" or they wouldn't be able to get married, then that would tend to indicate that she did *not* enter into it freely. Why not? Because there's no real choice in this matter, and even if there were, there would be no time to consult with a lawyer and make a rational, informed, and voluntary decision. This eleventh-hour tactic by Husband may even have been intentionally coercive and, under the law, should not be rewarded years later when the parties divorce.

The third issue is whether the distribution called for by the pre-nup is fair. This fairness must be assessed looking backward, at the time it was signed, and at the present, at the time of divorce. For example, regarding fairness at the time that the agreement was signed, the court may consider:

> the economic circumstances of the parties, the property brought to the marriage by each party, each spouse's family relationships and obligations to persons other than to the spouse, the earning capacity of each person, the anticipated contribution by one party to the education, training or increased earning power of the other, the future needs of the respective spouses, the age and physical and emotional health of the parties, and the expected contribution of each party to the marriage, giving appropriate economic value to each party's contribution in homemaking and child care services.[3]

That's a mouthful, to be sure. But there's even more. Remember, courts also have to assess fairness in the present tense, that is, at the time of the divorce. If things changed unexpectedly over the course of the marriage, the agreement may no longer be fair. For example, if Husband was worth $2 million, and the pre-nup limited Wife to only $500,000, that may no longer be fair now, even if it was at the time it was signed. Perhaps the couple was married for ten years, and Husband got lazy immediately after the wedding and stopped working, while Wife actually went out and earned most of the family income. Or perhaps Husband's $2 million in assets increased substantially over the course of the ten-year marriage, due in large part to Wife's efforts and contributions toward managing the assets. Perhaps the $2 million is now worth $10 million, and Wife's

$500,000 share under the pre-nup is not nearly adequate to compensate her for her hard work that led to the increase in the assets' value.[4]

So the pre-nup is by no means a slam dunk for the richer of the two parties. Further, it would be unlikely that a highly oppressive pre-nup—one that was forced on the other spouse and leaves him or her with next to nothing in the divorce—would be upheld in court. In fact, even if all the proper steps were taken to make the pre-nup a fair one at the time of signing, unforeseen events could render it unfair at the time of divorce.

Chapter 41
Can the government order you to pay support for someone else's child?

Yes. Surprisingly, the government can order a man to pay child support for a child that isn't even his.

Poor Mr. Smith. Married life was not all he had imagined, and after five unhappy years with his wife, he and Mrs. Smith agreed to divorce. During the time it takes for the divorce to make its way through the legal system, however, the soon-to-be ex-Mrs. Smith began a romantic tryst with Mr. Jones. Mr. Smith was unaware of the affair and didn't have a clue about what his wife was up to, until . . . she became pregnant.

When Mr. Smith found out about his wife's pregnancy, he *knew* that he was not the father, as he and Mrs. Smith hadn't been intimate for over a year. Yet, to his surprise, when Mrs. Smith finally gave birth to her child, an event that occurred long *after* the Smiths' divorce was finalized, the court demanded that Mr. Smith financially support the child! And if Mr. Smith were to refuse, his wages could be garnished, and he could even be convicted of a crime for failure to pay child support.[1]

How can this possibly be? Many states have what is called the "presumption of paternity" law, which is derived from the public policy against nonmarital children and, more specifically, the fear that these children will place a financial burden on the state. Therefore, the states that subscribe to such a presumption-of-paternity approach will simply *presume* that the man who was married to the woman, at the time she *became pregnant*, is the father. More precisely, the law reads:

Presumption of paternity: A man is *presumed* to be the father of a child if he and the child's mother are *or have been* married to each other and the child is *conceived or born* before the granting of divorce.[2]

And it's no easy task for Mr. Smith to "rebut" this presumption and convince the court otherwise. Why? Because the law places a heavy burden on Mr. Smith to show not only that he is *not* the father, but also that he knows who, specifically, the father really is.[3] Here's how it works: Mr. Smith can rebut the presumption that he is the father and get off the hook for child support, only if the court agrees to order DNA tests for him, the child, and the child's mother. This, of course, would prove that he's not the father. However, getting the court to order these tests is very difficult.

In this case, Mr. Smith would need to have a very specific set of allegations against Mrs. Smith. Just making a sworn statement that she has been unfaithful, and that he (Mr. Smith) is not the father, is not enough to get the court to order DNA testing. Instead, Mr. Smith would have to identify the man with whom Mrs. Smith had procreated and would need to be able to provide specific details about the intimate connection. Of course, this is probably information that Mr. Smith simply wouldn't have at his fingertips.

If Mr. Smith could not provide such specific information, the court might refuse to order DNA tests and might refuse to acknowledge any of Mr. Smith's claims or evidence that he is not the father. Why? Because it is not in the public's interest to have a nonmarital child on its hands, with no father to pay support. Instead, the court can simply saddle Mr. Smith with the financial responsibility, since his divorce from Mrs. Smith was not yet final at the time the child was conceived.

This dilemma is also relevant to married men whose wives conceive children by other men either during or even shortly *before* their marriage. The difficulty of obtaining court-ordered DNA tests will also be compounded if the married man initially acknowledged, and for some time raised and supported, the child as his own. Also, there is an additional problem: the presumption of paternity leaves the child's true biological father (in our example, Mr. Jones) without any legal rights regarding the child at all.[4] There are steps that the biological father can take to attempt to establish paternity, but in many real-life cases he is either unaware of the child or has chosen to avoid his moral responsibility, leaving the woman's husband or former husband on the hook for child support for years to come.

Taxes
Cuz I'm the Taxman

Chapter 42
If you find lost or abandoned property, do you have to pay taxes on it?

Yes.

Finding lost or abandoned property is known as finding a "treasure-trove," and the law says that it is a taxable event.[1] Why? Because the tax law was written very broadly and was purposefully drafted so that nearly all types of income qualify as gross income. And if something qualifies as gross income, then it is subject to federal income tax. More specifically, the law reads that "except as otherwise provided, gross income means *all income* from *whatever* source derived . . ."[2] And because finding a treasure-trove is *not* specifically *excluded* from gross income—that is, nowhere does the tax code say it should not be counted—then it *is* included in gross income and therefore is taxable.

Let's use an example adapted from the classic textbook case for treasure-trove income.[3] Suppose you buy a framed painting at a rummage sale. The painting is very old, but it isn't worth much money at all. It was painted by a no-name artist, really isn't all that attractive, and even the big, boxy frame is in pretty rough shape. But you like the color scheme and think it would go nicely in your living room, so you buy it for the small sum of twenty-five dollars.

When you get it home, however, instead of hanging it on your living room wall, you forget about it, and it ends up sitting in the basement with the rest of your junk. In fact, it sits there collecting dust until five years later when you clean out your basement. At that time, you "rediscover" the painting and decide you'll finally hang it up as you had intended. First, however, you're going to reframe it and get rid of the big, tacky frame.

When you start to take the painting out of the frame, you are surprised to find a very large, old envelope sandwiched between the frame's backing and the painting itself. You take it out and open it up, and inside you find $25,000 in cash! You can't believe what you're seeing. You know the money isn't yours, but you can't possibly return it; after all, you don't even remember where you bought that piece of junk painting to begin with. So you wisely check with your lawyer, who researches the law in your state, and he tells you that according to the law the money is yours. So the good news is that you've got $25,000. The bad news, however, is that you've got $25,000. Why is that bad? It's still better than not having $25,000, but unfortunately you're going to owe taxes on your newfound wealth.

The law says that finding a treasure-trove "constitutes gross income for the taxable year in which it is reduced to undisputed possession."[4] Further, in most jurisdictions, the date that you actually discover the treasure-trove is the date that it is "reduced to undisputed possession."[5] Therefore, the year you actually found the money in the painting, and *not* the year you bought the painting, is the year in which you'll owe taxes on the $25,000 in cash.[6]

In this case, it would be pretty simple, although somewhat painful, to pay your tax bill and retain the rest of the money from your so-called treasure-trove. But things can get really interesting when your treasure-trove consists of property and not cash. This was brought to light recently in major league baseball, when slugger Barry Bonds was nearing his 756th home run to top previous home run king Hank Aaron. For the person who caught that record-breaking home run ball, what are the tax consequences of the lucky grab?

Many tax experts believe that snagging such a valuable ball is the legal equivalent of finding a treasure-trove, and therefore it is taxable when you catch it because that is the point in time that you actually take legal possession of it.[7] Under that interpretation, if the fair-market value of the ball is $500,000, that must be included as income to be taxed in the year that the lucky fan catches the ball. Of course, this would make it impossible for anyone, except for the richest among us, to actually *keep* the ball. Instead, the sheer amount of the tax bill, based on the estimated fair-market value of the ball, would likely force the owner to sell the ball in order to pay the taxes.[8] Once the taxes are paid, of course, the balance of the selling price would be retained by the fan who caught, and then sold, the ball.

But what would happen if you're a really nice person and, upon catching the ball, wanted to give it back to good old Barry Bonds as a gift? Obviously, you wouldn't owe any taxes then, right? Don't be so sure. One IRS representative indicated that it would be taxable income to the person who caught the ball, and then that person could get hit with a big "gift tax" on top of it. However, in the face of public outcry from the baseball community, the IRS reversed this position for fear of looking like a bully.[9] But it's easy for the government to say that it wouldn't stick someone with a tax bill for gifting away a half-million-dollar baseball to the multimillionaire baseball player who smacked it out of the park. Everyone knows this would never happen anyway, so it's unlikely that the IRS would gain any real fans from its pseudogenerosity.

Chapter 43
If you barter for goods or services, do you have to pay taxes?

Yes.

As we saw in the previous chapter on taxation, the federal tax code starts with the general proposition that, unless specifically *excluded* from the category of taxable income, all income that you receive is taxable.

But bartering isn't income, right? After all, there's no money changing hands. In fact, the definition of bartering is "the trading of one product or service for another."[1] Before the start of our current monetary system, bartering was the only way business was done. In fact, people still barter today, even in economically advanced countries like the United States. But the fact is that, whether you are paid in cash or in goods or services, you are still earning income. You are providing a product or service, and you are getting something of value in exchange. True, you're not getting money, but you're still getting goods or services, and these definitely have value. Bartering, therefore, still produces taxable income.[2]

And you can probably imagine why the law is set up this way. Imagine for a moment how easy it would be to evade taxes altogether if bartering income were *not* taxable. For example, assume you're a plumber working in today's modern business environment, and you do some plumbing work for a homeowner who happens to be a carpenter. Normally, the carpenter would pay you in money (cash or check), you would report that money as income, and, depending on the amount of your deductible business expenses, you would pay the appropriate amount in taxes. Once that's done, you would then buy the goods or services you wanted with what's left of the money you earned.

However, you have a different proposal for your carpenter friend. Instead of a check or cash, you ask him to do the equivalent number of hours in carpentry work on your home. That way, he saves the cash, and you don't have to pay taxes on it. Everyone but the government would come out ahead. And that's precisely the reason it is illegal. (That, and another tip-off is that it's far too simple. If people could avoid taxes this easily, everyone would do it.)[3]

So, if you're ever wondering about whether something is taxable, it's often a safe bet to assume that Uncle Sam will get his income one way or the other. Of course, you can still do this type of barter exchange; there's nothing illegal about the exchange itself, provided that you claim the proper amount of taxable income and pay the proper amount of taxes. Again, just because you bypassed the cash portion of the transaction does not mean that it's tax free. But if it's not tax free, how do you go about paying taxes on it?

How the barter income should be reported and on which tax form may be tricky, depending on what you received and whether you were part of a formal barter club.[4] However, the amount to report is often straightforward. The amount of your taxable income from a barter exchange is the fair-market value of the goods or services you received.[5] Often, these will be the same for each person in the exchange, otherwise they wouldn't have bartered in the first place. And if the two people in the barter exchange agree ahead of time on the value of their products or services, then that amount will be considered the fair-market value, unless the value is determined to be otherwise.[6] Obviously, this is always subject to challenge by the IRS since the parties to the barter would have an incentive to understate the value of the services exchanged. Why? Because this would minimize the amount of taxable income for each party, which in turn would minimize their respective tax liabilities.

Before engaging in any bartering, however, be sure to check with your CPA or tax lawyer. In addition to the computation of taxable income, as well as the intricacies of how and where to report the income, barter income can, in some circumstances, require payment of a withholding tax. This is the prepayment of tax on a quarterly basis throughout the year, rather than at tax time. After all of these complications, you can see that it's far more convenient to simply deal in US currency.

Real Property Law
I Know What's Mine

Chapter 44
Is it possible to lose your property through "adverse possession"?

Yes. Oddly enough, it is possible to lose (or gain) legal ownership of real estate without selling (or buying) any property. One of the ways this can occur is by using the doctrine of adverse possession.

Adverse possession essentially means that someone who doesn't really own a particular piece of property may still acquire title to it—that is, come to own it over time—by using the property as if it were his own. This doctrine has a long, interesting, and very controversial history, in part because it may actually reward a trespasser by giving him legal title to the very property on which he was trespassing.[1]

There is, however, a bit more to the doctrine than simply using someone else's property. If it were that simple, everyone would do it and legal title to property would be changing hands all the time. Further, the doctrine varies a great deal from state to state, as well as by the type of property being adversely possessed. Typically, however, in order to gain ownership of another person's property through adverse possession, you would have to actually possess the property in a way that is hostile, exclusive, open, continuous, and under a claim of right.[2]

So what the heck does all of that mean? First, "actual possession" means that you are really possessing the property and acting like the owner of the property, even though in reality, you are *not* the owner. How do you do that? It depends on the type of property. If it is a vacant lot, for example, you may actually possess it by maintaining it and mowing the lawn. If it is a vacation home, you may actually possess it by using it during the summer months to relax on the weekends. In other words, you have to use the property in a way that is consistent with how the particular type of property would normally be used.[3]

Second, "hostile possession" means that you are possessing the property contrary to the true owner's interest. For example, if the property in question is a vacation home, and the true owner gives you permission to use his property from time to time for weekend getaways, then your possession is not hostile. Rather, it is with the true owner's permission. Under these circumstances, then, you could not gain title to the property; instead, you are merely an invited guest.[4]

Third, "exclusive possession" means that you are using the property while at the same time excluding others from using it. If, for example, there is a vacant lot at the end of your street, and you and all of your neighbors use it freely for picnics and other neighborhood activities, then you cannot gain title by adverse possession. Why not? Because your use of the property is not exclusive, and therefore you're not acting like how a true owner of the property would act.[5]

Fourth, "open possession" means that you are using the property openly, for everyone to see. In other words, you are not allowed to possess it covertly, with the intent of getting away with something. Going back to our vacation home example, suppose that you steal a key and sneak onto the property after dark to use the swimming pool for a few hours and then leave before sunrise. This type of use does not qualify as using the property openly, because others were not put on notice that you are claiming ownership.[6]

Fifth, "continuous possession" requires that you use the property continuously and for the statutorily prescribed period of time, which could range from only a few years to twenty years or even longer. If we return to our vacant lot example, let us assume that the statutory period of time for adverse possession is fifteen years. If you maintain the lot and use it in a way that is hostile, exclusive, open, and consistent with how vacant lots are used, but the true owner comes along and kicks you off his property after ten years, you would not have possessed the property continuously for the required period of time. Therefore, your claim of adverse possession would fail.[7]

Sixth and finally, you may also be required to possess the property under a "claim of right." In other words, you must be using or possessing the property with the good-faith belief that you are, in fact, the true owner of the property.[8]

With all of these requirements, how could anyone ever gain title to property through adverse possession? A common example is a boundary or property line dispute between neighbors. Suppose that you buy a house with a fence surrounding the backyard. You live there for twenty years, and you do all of the things that a home-owner would do on a property that he calls his home. This includes paying property taxes, using the backyard for recreation, and caring for the backyard by watering and mowing the lawn. Then, more than twenty years after you bought your home, your neighbor comes to you and says, "Hey, I just got a survey done, and your fence is on my property. In fact, it's six inches over, and I want you to move it, now!"

In this case, adverse possession may come to the rescue and save you from having to move your fence to give your neighbor back the six inches of land that is technically his. How? Well, you actually possessed the six-inch strip of land, which falls on your side of your fence, by using it, watering it, and mowing it. You also did so without his consent; in other words, your possession was hostile. Your possession was also exclusive—that is, no one else used your backyard as their own—and your possession was also open for all to see and was continuous for the statutory period of twenty years. Finally, you also possessed your neighbor's land in good faith. After all, the fence was there when you bought the house, you never had it surveyed, and you had every reason to believe that what was inside of the fence was yours and not your neighbor's.

This is precisely the type of situation for which the doctrine of adverse possession was designed. Given facts like these, you might very well prevail and acquire ownership of your neighbor's strip of land. In other words, your fence stays put.

Chapter 45
Is it possible to use your neighbor's property without trespassing?

Yes, sometimes it is possible. One way to do so is to acquire an easement on your neighbor's property.

Generally speaking, when a person owns land, he has the legal right to exclude others from his land; otherwise, there would be little benefit to owning the property in the first place. Conversely, if you were to go on someone else's land without her permission, you could be criminally or civilly liable for trespassing, under certain circumstances. However, there are some ways around this. One way to gain access to your neighbor's land is to acquire an easement on her property.

Although the precise definition will vary from state to state, an easement can be defined as "a nonpossessory interest in land that gives the holder the right to use land owned by another for a specific use and without profit."[1] In other words, an easement doesn't give you the right to possess—for example, take control of, or build a house on—your neighbor's property, but it would give you the right to *use* the property, without paying your neighbor, as long as you use it for the limited means specified in the easement document.

For example, suppose you own a piece of property, but the property is landlocked. That is, it is surrounded by property owned by other people—your neighbors—and you have no way of accessing your property from a public road without trespassing on one or more of your neighbors' pieces of property. So how can you get onto your own property under these circumstances? You could get an easement that allows you access to one of your neighbor's driveways, for example, for the purpose of getting to and from your property. Although easement documents can be very long and complex, here's an example of how the relevant portion of such an easement might be worded:

> NEIGHBOR hereby grants an easement and right-of-way to YOU, as well as to your successors and assigns, to use NEIGHBOR'S driveway as a joint driveway for ingress and egress to YOUR property. This right extends to YOUR personal, noncommercial use, as well as use by your guests and visitors that come to YOUR property for noncommercial purposes.

Of course, a good easement document would be drafted to comply with all state and local laws, and would also be thorough enough to address such things as: Who pays to maintain, insure, and repair the property governed by the easement? How are risks allocated in the event that you or your neighbor, or a third party, are injured while using the easement? Does the easement expire after a certain period of time or after a certain period of nonuse by you, the easement holder? These and other questions must be adequately answered in order to avoid disputes between you and your neighbor down the line.[2]

Now that we know what an easement is, how do we go about getting one? There are a number of ways of obtaining an easement. The simplest one is to pay for it. Just as you can buy the complete interest in a piece of land—assuming, of course, that the owner is willing to sell it to you—so too can you buy a lesser interest, such as an easement, in the same piece of land. In fact, easements often start out by stating: "For good and valuable consideration, the receipt and sufficiency of which are hereby acknowledged, the parties agree as follows . . ."[3] The cost of acquiring an easement can typically range from nominal sums of a couple hundred dollars, to many, many thousands of dollars. Much like buying the complete interest in a piece of property, it all depends on how badly the buyer wants or needs the easement, and how willing the owner is to sell the easement rights.

Another way to gain an easement is through the doctrine of necessity. Take, once again, our earlier example where you cannot gain access to your property without trespassing on your neighbor's land. You might be able to qualify for an easement by necessity if:

(1) at one time, there was a single, common owner of both your property and your neighbor's property; (2) that owner severed the property into the two properties that exist now—yours and your neighbor's; (3) your property had no access to a public roadway at the time it was severed; and (4) you still don't have access to a public roadway at the time you are seeking the easement.[4] Under these circumstances, you may be entitled to your easement because the land would be of no value without it, and it is therefore necessary for the basic enjoyment of the property.

Yet another way to obtain an easement is prescriptively, or through adverse possession. We saw in the previous chapter how it is possible to gain the complete and exclusive interest in a portion of someone's property through the doctrine of adverse possession. It is also possible, perhaps not surprisingly, to obtain a lesser property interest, such as an easement, in the same manner. If, for example, you had used your neighbor's driveway in such a way that was hostile, visible, open, notorious, continuous, and uninterrupted for the required period of time set forth in your state, then you could lay claim to having acquired the easement by adverse possession.[5] In that case, you would be able to continue to use the easement, without having to purchase the right, and without having to show necessity, or a need for the easement.

There are, of course, other ways to acquire an easement that are not addressed here. Further, regardless of the type of easement you acquire, the scope of the easement will likely be limited. For example, keeping with our earlier driveway easement, whether you acquired the easement by purchasing it, by necessity, by adverse possession, or by some other means, your permitted use of the property will likely be limited to driving on the driveway to go between your home and the public road. You would not be allowed, for example, to build anything on your neighbor's property, or grant anyone else permission to use it, except as specifically permitted in your easement agreement, if one exists.

Finally, very technical rules about proper documentation, notice, and recording of easements will likely apply, so consulting with a real estate attorney is a must before entering into any easement transaction.

Torts
Sue Happy

Chapter 46
Can you sue a restaurant if your coffee is too hot?

Possibly, but you'll need a bit more than just a piping hot cup of java.

The reality is that you can sue—that is, bring a "tort" action—in civil court for many different types of acts or omissions of others that cause you injury. There are two broad categories of civil torts: intentional and negligent. An example of an intentional tort is a battery. If someone were to walk up to you and punch you in the face, causing damages such as pain and injury, then you may very well have a civil cause of action for an intentional tort. In other words, you could sue that person for money because he intentionally caused you harm. (Additionally, the state may choose to file a *criminal* battery action against the perpetrator as well, which could result in incarceration, fines payable to the state, probation supervision, and court-ordered restitution to compensate you for your injuries.)

In the case of the piping hot coffee, however, it's unlikely that the restaurant deliberately turned up the heat on its coffee with the intention of harming you. Therefore, if you were to recover in a tort cause of action, it would likely be in the form of a negligent, rather than intentional, tort. To prevail in a negligence case, however, you would have to prove several things: first, that you suffered actual damages; second, that the restaurant breached its duty of care to you; and third, that its breach was the cause in fact, as well as the proximate cause, of your damages.[1] These elements may require more of an explanation.

First, you have to have actual damages. If your coffee is too hot, and the only consequence is that you can't drink it for ten minutes, you don't have any damages. However, if you were to burn yourself, then you have damages, the severity of which depends, of course, on the severity of the burn. Second, just because you were injured (burned) doesn't mean that you'll win your lawsuit. You'll also have to show that the coffee was unreasonably hot; that is, that the restaurant had a duty to brew coffee within a reasonable, acceptable temperature range, and it breached that duty by brewing the coffee at excessive temperatures.

Third and finally, you'll also have to prove that the restaurant's breach of its duty actually *caused* your injuries. This requires proof of cause in fact; that is, that the excessive temperature was at least a substantial factor in causing the burn. (That's easy enough in a case like this; what else, other than the heat, could have caused the burn?) But this also requires proof of proximate cause; in other words, that the burn was the natural and probable consequence of the excessive heat, and was not too remote of a possibility. (There are other complicating issues and defenses, but we will leave the analysis at this level for our purposes.)

This chapter's question stems from the famous McDonald's coffee-burning case. In this case, a civil negligence suit was brought against the McDonald's fast-food chain, claiming that the excessively hot coffee served by the restaurant caused severe burns to a customer. Many people have wondered how the plaintiff was able to win, and many people believe that the case epitomizes our litigation-happy culture. However, many misconceptions still remain regarding this fifteen-year-old case, and a closer look at the facts may be helpful and revealing.

In the McDonald's case, the plaintiff, seventy-nine years old at the time of the injury, was in the passenger seat of a stopped vehicle when she accidentally spilled the approximately 180 degree coffee into her lap. Coffee at other fast-food restaurants was generally served at least 20 degrees cooler, and coffee brewed at home is generally about 40 degrees cooler.[2] It was this high temperature of the coffee that accounted for the severity of the plaintiff's burns, which were third-degree burns over 6 percent of her body, including the particularly painful genital region.[3]

The plaintiff's injuries required a seven-night hospital stay, where she underwent skin grafts and other medical procedures.[4] The burns and the subsequent necessary medical treatment caused her pain, weight loss, and permanent scarring. They further resulted in costly hospital bills and loss of wages for the plaintiff's daughter who was the primary caretaker during the plaintiff's several weeks of recovery.[5] Perhaps most significantly, the McDonald's Corporation had numerous complaints on file about coffee burns in the ten years prior to the incident, including several second- and third-degree burns. The company had settled a number of these claims out of court for a significant amount of money.[6]

McDonald's was aware that the 180 degrees at which its coffee was served was near the high end of the temperature range for coffee; further, it was aware that such temperatures could cause severe burns. However, instead of changing its coffee-brewing policy, the McDonald's Corporation continued to enforce the requirement that each of their franchises brew and serve coffee at this high temperature.[7]

McDonald's was given, but refused, several opportunities to settle out of court, the first being the plaintiff's request to simply have her hospital bills and caretaker's lost wages paid. Instead, McDonald's offered only a fraction of these costs, forcing the plaintiff, who had never before sued anyone in her long life, to hire a lawyer to help recover her costs.[8] The jury members that were interviewed after the verdict admitted to being skeptical of a case about coffee burns. As the trial progressed, however, they became convinced that McDonald's had acted carelessly and with more concern for profits than for customer safety.[9]

Some of the most damaging evidence even came from those testifying on McDonald's behalf. One example is the McDonald's executive who testified that the restaurant, although aware of the resulting burns at the 180 degree temperature, had opted against a sterner warning to customers, claiming that "there are more serious dangers in restaurants."[10]

After seven days of hearing extensive evidence and testimony, the jury returned a verdict against McDonald's. Those who applaud the verdict have argued that the jury took all the right factors into consideration when rendering its decision and awarding damages to the plaintiff.[11] In other words, the plaintiff proved all of the elements. First, she proved severe damages in the form of pain, injury, and financial loss. Second, she proved that McDonald's breached the duty of care; that is, it kept its coffee well above the acceptable temperature range. Third and finally, she proved proximate cause; that is, the burn was foreseeable, and not too remote, as McDonald's had already received many complaints from other burn victims in recent years.

Therefore, many contend, the McDonald's coffee burning case, far from being an example of a frivolous lawsuit, actually embodies the correct treatment of a civil negligence case. That is, the jurors heard all the evidence, made their decision based on the breach of the duty of care and the resulting damages, awarded a fair amount in compensatory damages that took into account the partial liability of the defendant, and awarded punitive damages of only two days' worth of McDonald's coffee sales.[12]

Although the amount of punitive damages awarded was later adjusted to a lower number by the presiding judge, and adjusted downward again in a private arrangement between the plaintiff and the defendant, the McDonald's coffee case continues to be one of the most famous, interesting, and sometimes misunderstood cases in American civil law.

Chapter 47
Can a burglar sue me if he gets injured on my property?

Possibly, but it depends on the circumstances surrounding the injury.

As we discussed in other chapters, when a person is injured by another individual, he may file a civil tort case against that individual for money damages or for other remedies. These cases can be filed as either an intentional tort (deliberate wrongdoing on the part of a defendant) or a negligent tort (inadvertent wrongdoing on the part of a defendant who should have reasonably foreseen the harm caused by his negligent act). However, if a burglar breaks into someone's property and gets injured during the course of his unlawful act, the burglar in most cases would not be successful in a negligence lawsuit against the property owner. The reason is that in the United States, a property owner typically has a limited "duty of care" (one of the elements of a negligent tort) toward would-be burglars or trespassers.[1]

The operant phrase, of course, is "in most cases." One notable exception of a civil negligence suit brought by an alleged trespasser is the 1983 case *Bodine v. Enterprise High School*. In that case, a nineteen-year-old allegedly trespassed on the property of a high school in order to steal a floodlight. After allegedly unhooking the light and lowering it to his accomplices on the ground, the trespasser was walking on the school's roof and fell through an unseen skylight. As a result of the fall, he was diagnosed as a "spastic quadriplegic," a lifelong, life-changing, irreversible condition.[2]

The *Bodine* case has been debated by both sides of the tort reform movement, and the facts are often different depending on who is telling the story.[3] Many people who retell the story claim that it was the property's lack of posted warnings that was the loophole, allowing the case to proceed. However, others contend that this case was not filed as a "failure to warn" incident; that is, the plaintiff's suit did not focus on the lack of warning signs on the roof. Instead, the *Bodine* case was predicated on the alleged negligence in the design, construction, and operation of the skylight, which was painted a dark color that, in the dark of night, made it almost indistinguishable from the other parts of the roof.[4] The case was eventually settled out of court.[5]

The *Bodine* case, in many respects, is uncommon in United States law. In most other situations, recovering money for a negligent-related injury sustained while the plaintiff was committing a crime against the defendant is very, very difficult. However, there have been attempts to circumvent the legal elements of negligence (duty of care, foreseeable injury, and proximate cause) in these types of cases. An excellent example is the case of *Klein v. National Railroad Passenger Corp.*, in which two seventeen-year-olds used the "attractive nuisance" argument to sue for severe burns sustained while trespassing on the roof of a parked railroad car.[6]

The attractive nuisance concept is a doctrine of tort law aimed at preventing injuries to young children who trespass into dangerous areas or situations to which they are naturally drawn. Most people would not think that this concept, which holds the landowner liable for conditions hazardous to trespassing children, would apply to two young men just shy of their eighteenth birthdays.[7] However, a Pennsylvania federal judge ruled otherwise. Specifically, the judge stated that "seventeen-year-old males generally do not have fully mature brains, and as such cannot fully control their impulses or appreciate some risks."[8] The judge also ruled that the case met all five elements of the attractive nuisance doctrine, despite the defense's argument to the contrary.[9] Some have found the judge's decision very surprising, since the two plaintiffs were well past the age at which Pennsylvania law finds minors "presumptively capable of negligence," and therefore accountable for their own risk-taking behaviors.[10]

The *Bodine* and *Klein* cases, of course, are exceptions to the general tenets that prevent burglars and adult (or near-adult) trespassers from suing property owners for negligence. However, there is yet another type of lawsuit brought against property owners where would-be burglars allege intentional, rather than negligent, harm. Though most courts will uphold the right of a property owner to protect his family, possessions, and land from wrong-doers, some would-be burglars have sued property owners for using excessive or deadly force to stop them.

One well-known lawsuit of this nature is the 1971 case *Katko v. Briney*. In this case, when an intruder attempted to unlawfully enter an unoccupied house, a spring gun that the owner had mounted to stop just such an intrusion shot the trespasser in the leg. The jury ruled in favor of the injured trespasser-turned-plaintiff, reasoning that the deadly force of the shotgun was not reasonable for the protection of unoccupied property. However, the use of such force might be justified in some cases, for example, where a homeowner is in the house at the time of the intrusion and reasonably fears for his life or for the safety of his family.[11]

Still, being in one's house at the time of a break-in does not necessarily stop a would-be burglar from suing the homeowner. In a 2006 case, *Prochaska v. Rainiero*, an intruder sued a homeowner, alleging that the homeowner used excessive force in stopping him, despite the homeowner's claim that he fired in self-defense and that he feared for the lives of his wife and children.[12] In fact, the intruder sought damages for alleged injuries including "relentless pain" and "loss of earning capacity," although the intruder's case against the homeowner was subsequently dismissed at the trial-court level.[13]

The lesson is that these cases, much like other areas of United States law, are intensely fact-and-circumstance driven. In other words, no single factor is likely to provide a complete defense. Rather, it depends on the weight of all of the facts and circumstances surrounding the injury.

Chapter 48
Can I be sued for helping someone during an emergency?

Yes, possibly, depending on the specific circumstances.

This legal issue is related to the Good Samaritan laws that are in effect around the country. Although the basis for these laws is to protect individuals who help others during an emergency, the elements that need to be in place in order for a citizen to be "covered" by the Good Samaritan statutes are different throughout the United States.[1]

The uncertainties about what constitutes a Good Samaritan type of act can, in theory, lead to inaction. Take, for example, Stella. Stella is driving home from work when she sees the car in front of her veer off the road and hit a tree. She immediately pulls up behind the car, which contains two now motionless people. Stella wants to help—the people in the car may be severely injured—but doesn't know whether, legally, she is allowed to help them. This indecision on Stella's part is what many Good Samaritan statutes across the country are hoped to resolve. However, since the statutes vary, sometimes widely from state to state, the issue can still be a gray one. Furthermore, since Stella is not familiar with her state's statute, she may fear that she could be legally liable for any action she takes.

While reading this chapter is *not* a substitute for learning the exact Good Samaritan statutes for the state in which one lives, it aims to provide a sense of what kinds of "helpful acts" are covered by some of the Good Samaritan statutes. First of all, no matter where Stella lives, she should call 911 to get professional help on the way immediately. After that, there are a number of issues Stella should keep in mind:

Where do you live? There are a limited number of states where Stella has a "duty to rescue," that is, she must offer help to those in emergency situations as long as she does not endanger her own safety by doing so. These states are the exception rather than the rule, and in some of them, just the simple act of calling 911 fulfills this duty. In others, the duty is only triggered under very specific factual circumstances.[2]

Does the situation constitute an emergency? If an accident occurs or dangerous situation arises, but it is clear to a reasonable person that no life is in immediate danger, then it does not necessarily constitute an "emergency," and Stella's intervention might make her liable in a civil tort action if she causes further injury. This is currently the issue in a California case where a woman is being sued for dragging a friend from a car crash. The would-be Good Samaritan, worried that the car would explode with her injured friend inside, pulled her from the car. The friend, however, asserts that the act of being pulled from the car may have contributed to her permanent paralysis. Because the California Supreme Court determined that the situation did not actually constitute an emergency, the would-be Good Samaritan is not protected by the state's Good Samaritan law, and therefore can be sued civilly by the injured party.[3]

Do you have consent from the injured party (or, if the individual is a minor, from that child's parents or guardian)? If the injured individual is an adult and is unconscious, there may be "implied consent." This can also be true if the injured person is incapable of making a reasonable decision, for example, due to being drunk or mentally incapacitated. Consent can also be implied if the parent or guardian of an injured minor is similarly incapacitated. In any other case, Stella would need to make sure she gets the injured person's consent before she begins helping him, or she could well be held legally liable for any further injury to that individual.[4]

Are you providing the assistance voluntarily, i.e., with no expectation of payment or reward? In the case of Good Samaritan statutes covering the average citizen (as opposed to those statutes aimed at trained healthcare professionals), most require that the citizen must offer help "in good faith," without any expectation of payment or other compensation. Even accepting a "reward" after the fact may impact protection under a Good Samaritan law, in some cases.[5]

Do you have training in administering emergency healthcare? Using our earlier example, we may ask whether Stella is an off-duty physician. This is a factor to consider for at least two reasons. First, Good Samaritan statutes in some states specifically protect only skilled professionals (and not the average citizen), while in other states the laws are broadened to include the rest of us.[6] And second, an untrained layperson who makes a mistake attempting to administer CPR, for example, would not be liable under most Good Samaritan laws, but a trained professional who performs this same act incorrectly (and should have known better) could be liable if something goes wrong.[7]

Did you act only within (and not beyond) your skill level? This is loosely related to the issue above. For example, if Stella is a physician and decides to perform an emergency tracheotomy on a dying accident victim, she is likely acting within her skill level. This would not be the case for the average passerby, for whom such an act would be extreme and dangerous and clearly beyond a layperson's skill level.[8]

Did you act with reasonable care, and not in a significantly neglectful manner? That is, were any of the would-be Good Samaritan's acts grossly negligent, by the standard of a reasonable person in the same situation? For example, if Stella knows that she is highly intoxicated and still attempts to aid the injured party, any added injury that she causes through her actions could be considered the result of gross negligence.[9]

Once you began helping, did you continue to help until the situation was resolved? This is also connected to the "reasonable action" standard above. Once Stella begins to aid an injured individual, then she cannot stop unless she becomes too physically fatigued to go on, or a skilled professional takes over, or the injured individual recovers. To do otherwise could be considered an unreasonable act.[10]

Did you create the harmful or injurious situation? If Stella had in some way caused the car in front of her to crash, some states would consider her to have a "duty to rescue" those who were injured or imperiled by the situation she created.[11]

Do you have a duty of care toward the injured individual due to a "special relationship"? These special relationships may include the duty spouses have to each other, the duty property owners have toward invited guests, and the duty parents (or those acting in the place of parents, such as school officials or caregivers) have toward children who are still minors.[12] Once again returning to our example, if it was Stella's husband who was driving in front of her and was involved in the accident, she might be legally compelled to help him due to the nature of their relationship.

The obvious problem with Good Samaritan laws is that they vary from state to state, and usually involve the application of complex legal factors. However, in the real world, the types of situations that would invoke the Good Samaritan laws usually require snap decision making.

Chapter 49
People are spreading rumors about me— can I sue them for slander?

Yes. However, in order to win a slander case against someone, you would have to prove more than just the rumors.

First, both slander and a related cause of action—libel—fall under defamation law, which is a type of personal injury law. Slander and libel are very similar to one another: both occur when false and damaging information about someone is communicated to another person who believes the information. In fact, slander and libel differ in only one aspect: in slander, the derogatory statement is spoken, while in libel, the derogatory statement is written.[1]

Slander and libel have been legally actionable offenses since the inception of this country. In fact, the plot of a great 1930s Hollywood film, *Libeled Lady*, turns on this very issue: the plot revolves around a young socialite's libel suit brought against the newspaper that had accused her of home-wrecking. In this film—a film that is a romance and a comedy, but not a legal tutorial—the newspaper's publishers actually realized their mistake and stopped distribution of the accusatory edition. Unfortunately, this was not accomplished until *after* a few of the copies had been delivered. Even these few copies—in fact, even a single copy—can qualify. In the film, as in real life, that is enough to allow the libel suit to proceed.

Slander—the kissing cousin of libel—is defined as speaking a disparaging statement instead of writing such a statement. In both cases, however, the statement needs to be overheard by at least one other person, and that person has to believe that the statement is true.[2] Let's use a hypothetical example to illustrate how easy it is to become embroiled in a slander lawsuit. We'll also use the example to discuss what elements the plaintiff must prove in order to win a slander case, and what defenses the accused may use to defend such a case.

In our example, Leo is fed up with his coworker Cheryl. One day at the office he vents about Cheryl to a group of fellow employees, claiming Cheryl is an incompetent and unethical coworker who has been stealing company property including staplers, reams of printer paper, and boxes of pens. Leo feels better after he vents, but the situation is far from over. Cheryl hears from some fellow employees about Leo's outburst. Some other employees begin to treat her with contempt, and a week later she is turned down for a promotion by one of the very people who overheard Leo's harmful statements about her.

Cheryl now has everything she needs to bring a slander suit against Leo. Cheryl has the witnesses to confirm that: (a) Leo made the defamatory statement that was clearly about Cheryl and not some other person; (b) the statement was overheard by another, or others; and (c) one or more persons believed the statements to be true. The only other thing Cheryl would need to prove is that Leo's statement injured her reputation or caused some personal or monetary loss,[3] which could be supported by Cheryl's failure to gain the promotion.

Leo, of course, has the right to defend himself against Cheryl's suit, although in Leo's situation, only one of the four defenses against defamation would be applicable. The most obvious defense in a defamation case is truth, which is considered an "absolute defense" as long as Leo can prove that Cheryl had, in fact, been performing substandard work and stealing from the company.[4]

There are other defenses in defamation cases, but none that would likely help Leo in this scenario. One such defense would be to argue that the plaintiff consented to the statement.[5] Another defense is that the statement was made during testimony in court, which could be considered a "privileged statement," and therefore outside the scope of a slander claim.[6] Last, "innocent dissemination" of defamatory statements can also be a defense.[7] A simplified example of this is where a messenger transmits a sealed note between the CEOs of two different companies, which warns not to hire a job candidate, citing unproven allegations. In that case, although the CEO writing the message could be found guilty of libel, the messenger delivering the note could not, as he was "innocent" of the contents of the letter.

With regard to damages, many states are *per se* states, meaning that the state recognizes certain types of slander to be so serious that the plaintiff does not have to prove that the statement caused actual damages or was uttered with malice.[8] Statements that might fall into the *per se* category, depending on the state, could include those that accuse a person of being an embezzler or of having a "loathsome disease."[9] However, even in these *per se* states, there is no guarantee of big money for the plaintiff. In fact, although the jury may be required to return a verdict for the plaintiff, it is not required to award any set or minimum amount of damages.[10]

But what about freedom of speech and freedom of the press, also known as our First Amendment rights? Wouldn't that protect one from slander and libel lawsuits? Not so. First, while all citizens are protected under our crucial First Amendment rights, all "ordinary citizens" are also entitled to freedom from defamation.[11] To ensure maintenance of First Amendment rights, however, public officials or public figures who wish to bring suits for slander or libel are required to prove an additional element: that of "actual malice" on the part of the defendant. That is, while "ordinary citizens" still need to prove that a defamatory statement is untrue, a public figure would *also* need to prove that the defendant *knew* the defamatory statement was untrue.[12]

Legal Education
So You Want to Be a Lawyer?

Chapter 50
Do you have to go to law school to be a lawyer?

No. At least, not in some states.

Perhaps one of our country's most famous lawyers is our sixteenth president, Abraham Lincoln. His intelligence, dedication, and sense of justice are legendary. As a lawyer who practiced before the time that attorneys' work became "specialized," Lincoln worked for over twenty years as a general practice lawyer serving the citizens of Illinois on a wide variety of cases.[1] In fact, the excellent film *Young Mr. Lincoln*, starring Henry Fonda, focuses not on Lincoln's presidency but on his work as a lawyer. The film bases its fictional story on Lincoln's real-life defense (ending in acquittal) of accused murderer William Armstrong.[2]

Mr. Lincoln never went to law school.

In the state of Illinois during Lincoln's time, a prospective lawyer would prepare for the practice of law by studying law books on his own and learning under the supervision of licensed attorneys. This method was called "reading the law" and was the way that one moved from being an aspiring lawyer to a full-fledged member of a state bar organization before the prevalence of law schools.[3] This method obviously worked well for Lincoln, who was not only one of history's greatest orators and American presidents, but was also a great attorney.

Today, however, it is much more difficult to take Lincoln's path. Instead, attending law school is often thought of as a prerequisite to becoming an attorney. In fact, law schools, having recently exploded in number and size, are seemingly everywhere. There are now nearly two hundred accredited law schools—that is, schools that are approved by the American Bar Association (ABA)—across the United States.[4] And virtually all who aim to practice law in this country will first attend and graduate from an ABA-approved law school, and then take and pass their state's bar exam. However, what most people don't realize is that the first step in this process— attending and graduating from an ABA-approved law school—is not always required.

While most states *do* require aspiring attorneys to first earn their Juris Doctor degree (the degree awarded by law schools) before they can take the bar exam, a few states allow alternate paths. In fact, seven states—Vermont, New York, Washington, Virginia, California, Maine, and Wyoming—offer such options.[5]

For example, in California, one can qualify to take the bar exam by first reading the law for a period of years. This is done by one of two methods: the first is by "attending a law school approved by the State of California to award professional degrees but is unapproved by the State Bar of California (including online law schools)"; the second method requires "participating in an approved course of study in a law office or the chambers of a judge."[6] An individual who fulfills one of these two requirements, and then successfully passes the California bar exam, qualifies for admission to the bar as a licensed attorney. However, the California bar exam is one of the more difficult state bar exams and has one of the country's highest failure rates.[7] This makes it a true challenge to pass the bar without formal legal training at a law school.

As another example, Vermont State Supreme Court Justice Marilyn Skoglund passed the bar exam after "reading the law."[8] Vermont allows a person to sit for the bar after meeting certain educational and "moral" requirements, in addition to meeting age and citizenship requirements.[9] These requirements include, for example, "earning a bachelors degree from an accredited institution"; and undergoing "a criminal and financial background check."[10] Candidates also have to pass the Multistate Professional Responsibility Exam, the intention of which is to "measure the examinee's knowledge and understanding of established standards related to a lawyer's professional conduct."[11]

The process of becoming a lawyer without first going to law school can be lengthy and rigorous. And although "reading the law" is no longer the norm, as it was in Lincoln's day, it is still possible as long as the prospective "law reader" thoroughly researches the requirements of his or her state and state bar association. Therefore, "reading the law" should not be ruled out by aspiring young lawyers who want to go "old school"—or more accurately, "no school"— just as President Lincoln did.

Chapter 51
Do you have to pass the bar exam to be a lawyer?

Almost always, with one exception. There still remains one state where you don't have to "pass the bar" to become a lawyer.

Currently in the United States—in fact, in all states—to become a licensed attorney you have to first be admitted to a state's bar organization. Getting to that point usually requires graduating from law school, and almost always requires passing a state's bar exam. What is a bar exam? A bar exam is a broad-based examination that law school graduates must pass in order to be licensed to practice law in their state.[1] The bar exam is offered over a two- to three-day period and tests the examinees in areas of general legal principle and state-specific law. Most states also require a component called the Multistate Bar Examination that is composed of standardized questions on major areas of law, including contracts, torts, and evidence, among others.

However, there is still one state that honors what is called the "diploma privilege." For years, the diploma privilege existed in dozens of our states, but now exists only in Wisconsin. What is it? If you attend and graduate from one of the two accredited law schools in Wisconsin—that is, Marquette University Law School or the University of Wisconsin at Madison Law School—you automatically qualify for admission to the Wisconsin bar, and a license to practice law, *without* taking the Wisconsin bar exam.

Of course, this process is not as easy as it sounds. In addition to getting admitted to and then graduating from one of these two competitive law schools in Wisconsin, you'd also have to take certain classes to ensure the same knowledge base as someone who takes and passes the bar exam. For example, to be eligible for the diploma privilege, students from both Marquette University and the University of Wisconsin law schools must pass courses uniquely designed around Wisconsin law and legal procedures, as well as other specific subjects that are national in scope.[2]

At one time, more than thirty states offered the diploma privilege to graduates of their law schools.[3] In fact, by the second half of the nineteenth century, numerous states began offering the diploma privilege as a way to entice prospective law students to attend the law schools in their state.[4] The law profession itself, however, opposed this practice and thus due to pressure from legal organizations, states began dropping the diploma privilege.[5]

The last state to rescind its diploma privilege was West Virginia, which did so in 1988, leaving Wisconsin as the only state to retain it.[6] However, Wisconsin's retention of the diploma privilege is not without controversy and has been the subject of several legal challenges over the years. During one such challenge in the mid-1950s, the Committee on Legal Education and Bar Admissions referred to the findings of an earlier panel, which concluded that "the bar examination is an unnecessary and undesirable process."[7] Specifically, the committee did not feel that requiring Wisconsin law graduates to sit for the state bar would have the desired effect. Like those before and after it, the mid-1950s review committee rejected the notion that requiring the bar exam for its state's law graduates would help to weed out those unfit to practice law, given the high standards and rigorous training provided by both of Wisconsin's law schools.[8]

After resisting several attempts to overturn the diploma privilege over dozens of years, Wisconsin's law schools found the privilege once again under attack in recent years. In 2006, Steve Levine was elected as the State Bar of Wisconsin's new president.[9] One of Levine's goals was to either "abolish the bar exam or to extend it." In other words, Levine believes that no one or everyone should be required to take the exam.[10] Levine's position was recently bolstered by a class-action lawsuit filed in 2008, which claimed that Wisconsin's diploma privilege "discriminate[s] against out-of-state commerce, because of the facial differentiation between in-state and out-of-state law school graduates."[11] While the American Bar Association opposes the diploma privilege, the Wisconsin State Supreme Court has supported it, and this recent appeal will once again test the staying power of the privilege.[12]

The Wisconsin diploma privilege is certainly not a cut-and-dried issue. A number of students maintain that graduating from one of Wisconsin's law schools is more rigorous than passing the Wisconsin State bar exam. The Wisconsin Supreme Court's chief justice has said that the diploma privilege, instead of being considered out of date, should be considered progressive, and that other states might reinstate this privilege.[13] Other law professionals point out the vital benefits of the privilege, including increasing law student's attentiveness to issues of law not covered in the bar exam, and the retention of excellent lawyers within the state who might otherwise be tempted to accept jobs elsewhere.[14]

For now at least, if you can get accepted to one of Wisconsin's two law schools, Wisconsin might be an ideal place to study and practice law.

Chapter 52
Do all lawyers go to trial?

No. In fact, many attorneys have never even seen the inside of a courtroom (at least not professionally).

Many of our country's popular television shows and feature films inevitably show attorneys furiously battling it out in court, usually under the supervision of a cranky, no-nonsense judge. Examples of these television shows include *Boston Legal*, *Ally McBeal*, *The Practice*, and the wonderful but short-lived *Murder One*. Examples of popular films conveying this same image include *A Few Good Men*, *Laws of Attraction*, *My Cousin Vinny*, and even *Legally Blonde*. This pop culture image of the American lawyer, however, is not an accurate representation of the legal profession as a whole. While many attorneys do indeed appear in court, and some will even go to trial, many will not.

First, there is an important distinction to be made: even among attorneys who go into court, many will never have a trial. For example, criminal defense attorneys and district attorneys (prosecutors) will go to court and appear in front of judges for such proceedings as initial appearances, arraignments, motion hearings, plea hearings, sentencing hearings, and status conferences for ongoing cases. However, the vast majority of criminal cases, even for these courtroom lawyers, will resolve themselves through plea bargaining rather than by going all the way to a jury trial.[1]

On top of this, there are also civil cases—that is, disputes between individuals or between companies—that also play out in court, but again, usually do not make it all the way to trial. Such civil cases include divorce or custody issues, property disputes, personal injury cases, breach of contract disputes, and trust and estate litigation.

Of course, some of these court appearances, whether criminal or civil, may eventually lead to a trial. A criminal defense attorney, for instance, may go to court for a motion hearing to ask the judge to dismiss the charges against his client. However, if the judge rules against the defense attorney, and if no mutually acceptable plea arrangement can be reached with the prosecutor, the lawyers in that case may certainly find themselves in a heated jury trial.

In addition to all of these types of cases that take place in the courtroom but usually settle short of going to trial, there are numerous areas of law that play out *far* from the courtroom. In fact, if an attorney so chooses she can conduct a lifelong practice and never even set foot in a courthouse. These areas of practice commonly fall under the broad label of "transactional law."[2] Instead of going to court to argue after a dispute has developed, transactional lawyers will usually focus on preventing disputes in the first place. Their activities often include consulting with clients, drafting documents, planning and structuring business transactions, filing paperwork, and negotiating deals, to name only a few.

Sometimes these transactional lawyers are defined by the areas of law in which they practice, or specialize. For example, if a client—say, General Electric Corporation—wants to acquire another company, it would consult a mergers and acquisitions law firm to negotiate and carry out the deal. If IBM wants to issue more shares of stock, it would consult with a securities law firm to guide it through the process and ensure that the maze of federal and state law is complied with. And if a state government wants to raise money to fix its infrastructure, it would consult a government bond lawyer, or public finance lawyer, to carry out the transaction.

But transactional lawyers do not work solely for big businesses or government; individual clients use them as well. If a married couple, for example, wants to preserve their assets to pass on to their children, they would consult a trusts and estates lawyer to develop an estate plan and draft the necessary documents. If an individual business owner wants to protect himself from personal liability, he would consult a business lawyer to establish a small corporation or other legal entity. If a homeowner wants to sell his home, he may consult a real estate lawyer to review the offer to purchase, draft the deed, and ensure that the transaction goes smoothly. And if a foreign citizen wants to move to the United States, he would consult with an immigration lawyer in order to obtain the proper legal status.

Other times, transactional lawyers are identified not by the area of law they practice but rather by whom they are employed. In fact, rather than working for law firms, many lawyers will work directly and exclusively for their client. For example, corporations, universities, and government bodies and agencies at all levels will employ lawyers directly. In those cases, the lawyers may work on a broad range of legal matters, including day-to-day business transactions, but once again, they will never be seen in court.

Simply put, as a result of the growing complexity of our laws and regulations, we've developed an army of lawyers throughout the United States who work exclusively behind the scenes. This type of lawyer toils away diligently outside of the courthouse, and therefore is rarely featured in American television or film.

Chapter 53
Is becoming a lawyer the road to riches?

No, probably not; at least, not anymore.

Many decades ago, becoming a lawyer, like becoming a medical doctor, was thought to be the road to great wealth. For the vast majority of law students today, however, that view has changed dramatically. This change, in large part, is due to supply and demand, as evidenced by the dramatic increase in the number of law schools, law students, and lawyers in our country. So if you're a prospective law student whose primary motivation for considering law school is financial, then you should give strong consideration to other careers as well.

When deciding whether law school is a good *financial* decision, you have to consider at least three things: (1) the cost for tuition, books, and fees, including debt incurred; (2) the "opportunity cost" of attending law school; and (3) the future earnings you can expect to make. The first of these three factors is relatively straightforward. How much will law school cost you in tuition, books, fees, and other expenses? This amount will have to be paid somehow, usually by exhausting personal savings or by taking out loans and going into debt. But how much is it? It varies dramatically by school, and there may be big differences between the in-state tuition at a public university and the tuition at a private law school.

For example, an in-state resident attending law school at the University of Georgia can expect to pay just under $15,000 for tuition, fees, and books per year.[1] However, any student (whether an in-state or out-of-state resident) attending Emory University, a private law school in Georgia, can expect to pay more than $40,000 per year for tuition, fees, and books.[2] As another example, an in-state resident attending the University of Illinois Law School can expect to pay tuition and fees of more than $35,000 per year,[3] while any student (whether an in-state or out-of-state resident) attending Northwestern University, a private law school in Illinois, can expect to pay more than $45,000 per year.[4]

Obviously, these are huge dollar amounts. Law school is usually a three-year program, so if a school's tuition, fees, and books come to $30,000 per year, that's $90,000 for the total cost of the degree, not counting the inevitable annual tuition increase. But this is only the "sticker price," and doesn't include potential merit-based or need-based scholarship money. For example, at Marquette University in Milwaukee, the sticker price for tuition is about $31,000 per year.[5] However, Joe Zilber, a graduate of Marquette University, recently donated $30 million to the law school, of which $25 million will be used exclusively for scholarships.[6] Therefore, the actual price that a well-qualified applicant would pay may be much, much lower than the advertised sticker price. In fact, highly qualified applicants may very well receive a full-tuition scholarship at many schools, including those discussed in this chapter.

On average, however, the cost of law school for most students is staggering and is funded largely by taking on debt. The average total debt load for 2007 law school graduates who incurred debt ranged from more than $126,000 to less than $17,000, depending on the graduate's school.[7] Of course, these average debt loads include money that was borrowed to pay for living expenses while the student was in school and not working, which could vary dramatically by geographic location.

And you may not know the *true* cost of tuition, fees, and books, or the amount of your prospective debt load, until you apply and are accepted to your school of choice. Therefore, it may be a good idea to apply to a few schools, including some less competitive and less prestigious schools. Would you rather take on over a hundred thousand dollars in debt to go to an Ivy League law school, or receive a full-tuition scholarship at a less prestigious school in the South or Midwest? Unfortunately, you may not know your full range of financial aid options until you apply to a variety of schools and see what they offer you.

But there are costs other than tuition that must be considered as well. For example, if you want to go to law school full-time, you'll probably have to quit your job. That's income that you won't be able to earn, and that's three fewer working years that you'll have available to you. That is known as an "opportunity cost" because, if you choose to attend law school, you'll lose out on the opportunity to earn income for those years. (However, you may get the opportunity for summer employment while you're in law school, which could offset some or even all of the lost income.) Opportunity costs will vary dramatically from person to person. For example, if you're an established accountant earning $60,000 per year plus benefits, your opportunity cost of attending law school would be much *greater* than the recent college graduate who is unable to find any substantial employment. Why? Because you'd have a lot more to lose by going back to school.

And finally, there is the future salary that you'll expect to make as a lawyer. While some large, national law firms in big cities may offer starting salaries around $150,000 or more per year,[8] you need to know a couple of important caveats regarding this attractive number. First, these firms usually only interview graduates who rank in the top 10 to 20 percent of their law school class, depending on the prestige of the particular school. That will automatically exclude 80 to 90 percent of the graduates from even getting an interview, let alone a job offer. Second, most of the graduates who land one of these large firm associate positions will *not* progress to a partnership position. The reality is that most will either leave after a relatively short stint, due to the immense workload or other adverse working conditions, or will be terminated when it is determined that they are not partnership material. So even for the few graduates who want, and land, a big firm associate position, the job could well be far from permanent.

While any given graduate's actual salary will depend on class rank in law school, the area of practice, and the employer's size and location, among other factors, the reality concerning salaries is sobering. (This is especially true when considered in relation to average graduate debt loads.) A 2007 study put the median starting salary for law school graduates at $62,000 annually, with nearly 30 percent of all law school graduates earning only between $40,000 and $55,000 per year.[9]

So what does all of this mean? If you're an accountant earning $60,000 dollars per year, and you want to quit work to go back to law school so you can eventually earn $60,000 per year, you might want to think twice. If tuition and fees will cost you only $25,000 annually, that's a total cost of over a *quarter-million dollars* in tuition and lost income alone, just to earn the same salary that you're earning now. (This, of course, is only a rough estimate since it ignores several financial factors, including the "time value" of money, the taxes taken out of your salary if you stay at work, and tuition increases if you go back to school, to name only a few.)

While law school and the law have always been viewed somewhat romantically by Hollywood, the decision of whether to go to law school should be based, at least in part, on cold, hard, financial reality. Before anyone commits to attending law school in today's economic climate, he should do a thorough analysis and consider all of the costs and benefits before making a commitment.

Afterword

Though we just covered numerous areas of law—including criminal law, criminal procedure, contract law, tax law, and family law, to name only a few—the fact is that we've only just skimmed the surface of US law. Law in our country is incredibly vast and far-reaching. Every year our lawmakers—including state and federal legislatures, state and federal courts, and other governmental bodies and lawmaking authorities—reach further and further into our lives by piling up thousands upon thousands of pages of law in its various forms. And the old laws rarely go away. We're in such a rush to make new laws that we never do any "house cleaning" to get rid of the old ones. Instead, they linger there, waiting to jump out at us and impact our lives.

The point of all of this is that law cannot (and should not) be memorized. Perhaps by now you have gained additional insight into the process of legal reasoning. As you've seen, the law is usually flexible and fact-specific. Therefore, the ultimate answer to a legal issue is usually *not* reached by simply consulting a law book, but rather through the process of legal reasoning.

Lawyers and law professors like to shroud the process of legal reasoning in mystery and legalese. Law schools, for example, take great pride in teaching their students to "think like lawyers." The legal reasoning process is, however, nothing more than: (1) gathering all of the facts; (2) identifying the legal issue, that is, the question that the parties are fighting about; (3) locating the applicable rule of law; (4) applying the law to the facts; and (5) reaching a conclusion.

While this legal reasoning process may be straightforward in the classroom, it is often difficult to apply in practice. For example, the facts can be elusive. The legal issue may be a subtle one, or may contain several sub-issues. Finding the applicable rule of law in today's hyper-regulated world is often like looking for a needle in a haystack. And applying the rule of law to the facts is the most difficult part of all; it's what lawyers and judges get paid to do, yet sometimes they get it wrong.

Finally, what about the conclusion? Law professors will tell you that the conclusion is the *least* important part of your answer on a law school exam. That's easy to say when you're in school, but in the real world the ultimate conclusion can have a tremendous impact on real people. The conclusion or answer to even the smallest of legal issues could mean the difference between receiving no money at all and millions of dollars, between being incarcerated for decades or being granted instant freedom, or, in some states, between being sent to prison or being sentenced to death. All of this makes the law interesting, engrossing, and serious all at the same time.

By now, however, we've said enough. You've certainly read enough about the law to engage your interest. And for those particularly inspired, there is always the calling of the law to be pursued.

Endnotes

1

1. This language is an abbreviated version of an actual village ordinance, which reads: "Mashing: No person shall improperly accost, ogle, insult, follow, pursue, lay hands on or otherwise molest any person of the opposite sex." Further, the term "ogle" means "to eye amorously or provocatively." See http://www.merriam-webster.com/dictionary/ogle (accessed November 1, 2008).

2. If a person is convicted of disorderly conduct and has a sufficient prior criminal record, then he or she could receive a prison term instead of a jail term or a fine. Just one such example of this type of law is section 939.62 of the Criminal Code of the State of Wisconsin, which requires only three prior misdemeanor convictions in the last five years in order to send a person to prison for disorderly conduct. See http://www.legis.state.wi .us/statutes/Stat0939.pdf (accessed November 1, 2008).

3. This language is an abbreviated version of section 947.01 of the Criminal Code of the State of Wisconsin, http://www.legis.state.wi.us/ statutes/Stat0947.pdf (accessed November 1, 2008).

2

1. This language is a slightly modified version of section 346.63 of the Wisconsin Statutes, http://www.legis.state.wi.us/statutes/Stat0346.pdf (accessed November 8, 2008).

2. This definition of the term "operate" is taken from section 346.63(3)(b) of the Wisconsin statutes, http://www.legis.state.wi.us/ statutes/Stat0346.pdf (accessed November 8, 2008).

3. In fact, this example is based on the case of *Milwaukee Cty. v. Proegler*, 291 N.W.2d 608 (Wis. Ct. App. 1980), where the defendant was found asleep in his car with the heater on and the car in park.

4. In fact, this example is based on the case of *State v. Wolford*, 604 N.W.2d 35 (Wis. Ct. App. 1999), where the defendant was found asleep in his car with key in the ignition, turned, but with the engine off.

5. KARE 11 Minneapolis St. Paul, "Georgia Man Charged with DUI in Wheelchair," http://www.kare11.com/news/whatsup/whatsup_article .aspx?storyid=527026&catid=333 (accessed November 9, 2008).

6. *St. Petersburg Times* Online, "Woman's DUI Case Questions Definition of Vehicle," http://www.sptimes.com/2004/12/13/Hernando/ Woman_s_DUI_case_ques.shtml (accessed November 9, 2008).

7. *St. Petersburg Times* Online, "Judge Tosses Out DUI-Wheelchair Case," http://www.sptimes.com/2005/01/04/Hernando/Judge_tosses_out _DUI_.shtml (accessed November 9, 2008).

8. Ibid.

9. Ibid.

3

1. This language is based on section 940.19(1) of the Criminal Code of the State of Wisconsin, http://www.legis.state.wi.us/statutes/Stat0940 .pdf (accessed November 23, 2008).

2. This language is based on section 940.19(2) of the Criminal Code of the State of Wisconsin, http://www.legis.state.wi.us/statutes/Stat0940 .pdf (accessed November 23, 2008).

3. For an example of a self-defense statute, see section 939.48 of the Criminal Code of the State of Wisconsin, http://www.legis.state.wi.us/ statutes/Stat0939.pdf (accessed November 23, 2008).

4. Andrew S. Gold, *Absurd Results, Scrivener's Errors, and Statutory Interpretation*, 75 UNIVERSITY OF CINCINNATI LAW REVIEW 25 (2006), http://www.law.uc.edu/academics/docs/h-Gold.pdf (accessed November 23, 2008).

4

1. This chapter addresses the use of marijuana for some type of ingestion into the body. For a more detailed discussion of the legality of hemp products generally, see US Drug Enforcement Administration's "DEA Clarifies Status of Hemp in the Federal Register," http://www.usdoj.gov/dea/pubs/pressrel/pr100901.html (accessed November 18, 2008).

2. Nicole Watkins, "Explained: Why Are Ann Arbor's Pot Laws So Lax?" *Michigan Daily*, January 17, 2008, reprinted at http://www.marijuana.com/drug-war-headline-news/89333-mi-explained-why-ann-arbors-pot-laws-so-lax.html (accessed November 5, 2008).

3. Ibid.

4. See the Uniform Controlled Substances Act for prohibitions and penalties, http://www.legis.state.wi.us/statutes/Stat0961.pdf (accessed December 2, 2008).

5. Ibid.

6. See, for example, Gabriel J. Chin, *Race, the War on Drugs, and the Collateral Consequences of Criminal Conviction*, 6 JOURNAL OF GENDER, RACE & JUSTICE 253 (2002), http://papers.ssrn.com/sol3/papers.cfm?abstract_id=390109 (accessed December 2, 2008).

7. "State Medical Marijuana Laws," http://medicalmarijuana.procon.org/viewresource.asp?resourceID=881 (accessed November 5, 2008).

8. Ibid.

9. Sarah Crone, "Voters Approved Medical Marijuana," *Kalamazoo Gazette*, November 5, 2008, http://www.mlive.com/kzgazette/news/index.ssf/2008/11/voters_approve_medical_marijua.html (accessed November 5, 2008).

10. "Does a State's Medical Marijuana Laws Put That State in Violation of Federal Drug Law?" http://medicalmarijuana.procon.org/viewanswers.asp?questionID=634 (accessed November 5, 2008).

11. Ibid.

5

1. For an example of a case that stands for this proposition, see the case of *United States v. King*, 349 F.3d 964 (7th Cir. 2003).

2. For an example of a bond statute, which discusses both monetary and nonmonetary components of bond, and the factors that may be con-

sidered in setting conditions of bond, see Chapter 969 of the Criminal Code of the State of Wisconsin, http://www.legis.state.wi.us/statutes/Stat0969.pdf (accessed November 8, 2008).

3. For an example of a bail jumping statute, see Section 946.49 of the Criminal Code of the State of Wisconsin, which criminalizes any behavior that intentionally violates a condition of bond, http://www.legis.state.wi.us/statutes/Stat0946.pdf (accessed November 8, 2008).

4. For an example of a case where the defendant was released from custody on bond and was convicted of bail jumping for violating a "no contact" order by making a nonthreatening phone call from fifty miles away, see the case of *State v. Boho*, 568 N.W.2d 322 (Wis. Ct. App. 1997). The court confidently declared that the nonthreatening phone call "was a clear violation of that order."

5. In fact, virtually any bond condition will be upheld as valid, as long as it is "reasonable." This, of course, is an incredibly easy test to pass. For example, it can be reasonable for a court to order as a condition of bond that a defendant not consume alcohol, even when there was no alcohol or drug use involved in any way in the underlying crime with which the defendant is charged. For an example of this, see the case of *State v. Modrow*, 570 N.W.2d 61 (Wis. Ct. App. 1997).

6. A defendant is guilty of bail jumping if, "while released from custody" on bond, he or she "intentionally fails to comply with the terms of his or her bond." Whether the defendant is innocent or guilty of the underlying charge that gave rise to the bond in the first place is completely irrelevant. See Section 946.49 of the Criminal Code of the State of Wisconsin, http://www.legis.state.wi.us/statutes/Stat0946.pdf (accessed November 8, 2008).

6

1. For a common example of a disorderly conduct statute, see section 947.01 of the Criminal Code of the State of Wisconsin, http://www.legis.state.wi.us/statutes/Stat0947.pdf (accessed March 14, 2009).

2. Ibid.

3. Ibid.

4. Ibid.

5. Ibid.

6. For an excellent overview of disorderly conduct in the domestic set-

ting, including the numerous and harsh consequences that go along with it, see the Web site of law firm Van Wagner & Wood, S.C., http://www.van wagnerwood.com/CM/Custom/Domestic_Disorderly_Conduct.asp (accessed March 14, 2009).

7. For example, see section 939.62 of the Criminal Code of the State of Wisconsin, which requires only three prior misdemeanor convictions in the last five years in order to send a person to prison for disorderly conduct, http://www.legis.state.wi.us/statutes/Stat0939.pdf (accessed March 14, 2009).

8. Van Wagner & Wood, S.C., http://www.vanwagnerwood.com/CM/ Custom/Domestic_Disorderly_Conduct.asp (accessed March 14, 2009).

9. Eileen Hirsch, Ginger Murray, and Wendy Henderson, *Raise the Age: Return 17-Year-Olds to Juvenile Court*, WISCONSIN LAWYER 80, no. 6, June 2007, http://www.wisbar.org/AM/Template.cfm?Section=Search _Archive1&template=/cm/htmldisplay.cfm&contentid=65353 (accessed March 14, 2009).

10. Ibid., Figure 1, "Most Common 17-Year-Old Offenses," http:// www.wisbar.org/AM/Template.cfm?Section=Wisconsin_Lawyer &Template=/CM/ContentDisplay.cfm&CONTENTID=65278#f1 (accessed March 14, 2009).

7

1. This language is a slightly modified version of section 941.23 of the Criminal Code of the State of Wisconsin, http://www.legis.state.wi.us/ statutes/Stat0941.pdf (accessed April 25, 2009). See also Wisconsin Criminal Jury Instruction 1335 and accompanying commentary and notes.

2. This language is a slightly modified version of section 167.31(2)(b) of the Wisconsin statutes, http://www.legis.state.wi.us/statutes/Stat0167 .pdf (accessed April 25, 2009).

3. See Wisconsin Criminal Jury Instruction 1335, Comment, discussing the conflict between the two statutes.

4. *State v. Walls*, 526 N.W.2d 765, 768 (Ct. App. Wis. 1994).

5. *State v. Keith*, 498 N.W.2d 865, 866 (Ct. App. Wis. 1993) (internal citations omitted).

8

1. For a typical example of a statutory rape statute, see sections 948.02 (2) and 948.01 (5) of the Criminal Code of the State of Wisconsin, which makes it a felony to sexually touch a fifteen-year-old, even if the touching is on top of the minor's clothing, http://www.legis.state.wi.us/statutes/Stat0948.pdf (accessed November 30, 2008).

2. For an example of such a rule, see section 939.43 (2) of the Criminal Code of the State of Wisconsin, which reads that "A mistake as to the age of a minor . . . is not a defense." http://www.legis.state.wi.us/statutes/Stat0939.pdf (accessed November 30, 2008).

3. These facts were adapted from the case of *State v. Jadowski*, 680 N.W.2d 810 (Wis. 2004).

4. Ibid. at 817.

5. Some of these repercussions are a natural consequence of any felony conviction. However, convictions for sex crimes put defendants at risk for extremely draconian punishment and restrictions on their liberty. For example, there has recently been an explosion of sex offender registration laws at all levels of government, including local, state, and federal, which often severely restrict a person's residence and even their movement. For a more detailed discussion, see Bob Egelko, "Court: Sex-Offender Law Unfairly Restrictive," *SF Gate*, http://www.sfgate.com/cgi-bin/article.cgi?f=/c/a/2008/11/20/BAER149660.DTL&tsp=1 (accessed November 30, 2008).

6. For example, see Larry W. Myers, *Reasonable Mistake as to Age: A Needed Defense to Statutory Rape*, 64 MICHIGAN LAW REVIEW 105 (1965–66).

9

1. Sometimes, but not always, in order to convict a person of a crime the prosecutor may have to prove *not only* that the alleged victim did not consent to the particular act but also that the defendant *knew* that the alleged victim did not consent. This requirement may vary by state, and even by the type or degree of the criminal charge within a state.

2. For example, in the Criminal Code of the State of Wisconsin, sexual intercourse with a sixteen-year-old carries a maximum possible penalty of nine months in jail. However, if the child victim were only one day shy of sixteen, that is, still fifteen years old, then the maximum possible penalty

jumps to forty years in prison. See sections 948.02 (2), http://www.legis
.state.wi.us/statutes/Stat0948.pdf and 939.50 (3), http://www.legis.state.wi
.us/statutes/Stat0939.pdf (accessed February 6, 2009).

3. "Woman Received Oral Sex in Parked Car—Charged with Crime
against Nature," democraticunderground.com, http://www.democratic
underground.com/discuss/duboard.php?az=view_all&address=105x132
1140 (accessed January 31, 2009).

4. Ibid.

5. *Lawrence v. Texas*, 539 U.S. 558 (2003).

6. Ibid. (Emphasis added and internal citations omitted.)

10

1. Franklin Foer, "Adultery," *Slate*, June 15, 1997, http://www.slate
.com/id/1063/ (accessed February 8, 2009).

2. Ibid.

3. Liza Mundy, "Actually It Is a Crime," *Washington Post Magazine*,
February 22, 1998, http://www.washingtonpost.com/wp-srv/politics/
special/clinton/stories/mundy022298.htm (accessed February 8, 2009).

4. Foer, "Adultery."

5. Ibid.

6. Michigan Penal Code Section 750.29 Adultery; definition, http://
www.legislature.mi.gov/(S(k5chc445ase2s155anxf0u45))/mileg.aspx?page
=getObject&objectName=mcl-750-29 (accessed February 8, 2009).

7. "Adultery Is a Crime," http://www.adulteryisacrime.com (accessed
February 8, 2009).

8. New York Penal Code Section 255.17 Adultery, http://wings
.buffalo.edu/law/bclc/web/NewYork/ny3%28b%29.htm (accessed February 8, 2009).

9. Sewell Chan, "Is Adultery a Crime in New York?" *New York
Times*, March 21, 2008, http://cityroom.blogs.nytimes.com/2008/03/21/
is-adultery-a-crime-in-new-york/ (accessed February 8, 2009).

10. Foer, "Adultery."

11. Joanna Grossman, "Punishing Adultery in Virginia: A Cheating
Husband's Guilty Plea Is a Reminder of the Continued Relevance of Adultery Statutes," findlaw.com, December 13, 2003, http://writ.news
.findlaw.com/grossman/20031216.html (accessed February 8, 2009).

12. Ibid.

13. Ibid.
14. "Adultery Is a Crime."
15. Grossman, "Punishing Adultery in Virginia."
16. Mundy, "Actually It Is a Crime."
17. Grossman, "Punishing Adultery in Virginia."
18. Foer, "Adultery."

11

1. "Lawmakers Won't Legalize Prostitution in Vegas," Associated Press, reprinted in *Mercury News*, February 12, 2009, http://www.mercury news.com/news/ci_11689291 (accessed February 15, 2009).

2. Mike Leco, "Sex in Las Vegas," http://www.usatourist.com/ english/places/lasvegas/sex.html (accessed February 15, 2009).

3. David McGrath Schwartz, "Legislature Will Pass on Legalizing Prostitution in Las Vegas," *Las Vegas Sun*, February 12, 2009, http://www.las vegassun.com/news/2009/feb/12/legislature-will-pass-taxing-prostitution/ (accessed February 15, 2009).

4. Ibid.

5. Leco, "Sex in Las Vegas."

6. Joseph Abrams, "22-Year Old Sells Virginity On-line—and Feds Can't Do a Thing to Stop Her," January 12, 2009, http://www.foxnews .com/story/0,2933,480037,00.html (accessed February 15, 2009).

7. Leco, "Sex in Las Vegas."

8. Cecil Adams, "Why Is Prostitution Illegal?" straightdope.com, January 14, 2000, http://www.straightdope.com/columns/read/2533/why-is-prostitution-illegal (accessed February 15, 2009).

9. Ibid.

10. Emily Bazelon, "Why Is Prostitution Illegal? The Oldest Question about the Oldest Profession," slate.com, March 10, 2008, http://www.slate .com/id/2186243/pagenum/all/#p2 (accessed February 15, 2009).

11. Ibid.

12. Ibid.

13. Ibid.

14. Cynthia Needham, "Bill to Close Prostitution Loophole," *Providence Journal*, March 13, 2008, http://www.projo.com/news/content/ PROSTITUTION_BILL_03-13-08_1F9C07G_v10.372d934.html (accessed February 15, 2009).

15. "RI Gov Signs Bill Banning Indoor Prostitution," Associated Press, November 3, 2009, http://www.lasvegasnow.com/Global/story.asp?S=11435409 (accessed January 9, 2010).

12

1. See the case of *Miranda v. Arizona*, 384 U.S. 436 (1966). State courts may interpret a defendant's rights differently, but in no case can a state offer less protection than that afforded under *Miranda*. For example, the warning in the text was confirmed in the case of *State v. Mitchell*, 482 N.W.2d 364 (Wis. 1992).

2. For example, see the case of *State v. Hockings*, 273 N.W.2d 339 (Wis. 1979), where the court stated that "both custody and some form of questioning were necessary before *Miranda* warnings were required . . ."

3. For example, see the case of *Easley v. Frey*, 433 F.3d 969 (7th Cir. 2006), where the police told the defendant the charges against him and the potential sentence, thereby inducing the defendant to respond. For another example, see the case of *Cannady v. Dugger*, 931 F.2d 752 (11th Cir. 1991), where the police asked the defendant where he was on the night of the crime, also inducing him to respond. In neither case, however, was the police action considered to be an interrogation, even though the police in *Cannady v. Dugger* actually interrogated, or asked a question of, the defendant.

4. For example, see the case of *U.S. v. Courtney*, 463 F.3d 333 (5th Cir. 2006), which holds that when questioning occurs in a public place or at a place of employment, the defendant is not in custody and therefore *Miranda* warnings are not required before the police interrogate the defendant. For another example, see the case of *Joseph v. Coyle*, 469 F.3d 441 (6th Cir. 2006), where the court decided that the defendant was not in custody, even though the questioning occurred at the police station. The reasons were that the defendant came voluntarily to the police station, and he was never told that he was not free to leave.

5. The general rule is that the prosecutor, at a criminal trial, cannot comment on a defendant's choice to exercise a constitutional right, including the right to counsel. However, if the defendant were to testify at trial and assert that he "never had the opportunity to tell his side of the story," or that "the police never bothered to ask him his side of the story," for example, such a tactic may well "open the door" to the fact that the defendant refused to talk and instead requested an attorney. Arguably,

other situations could open the door as well, but that's too complicated for our purposes.

13

1. Hypertechnical factual differences determine whether "probable cause," or the lower standard of "reasonable suspicion," is required for law enforcement to detain a suspect. To make matters even more complicated, reasonable suspicion could at some point morph into probable cause. These subtleties are beyond our scope, however, and we will therefore focus on the concept of probable cause.

2. See the case of *Illinois v. Gates*, 462 U.S. 213 (1983).

3. *United States v. Patterson*, 65 F.3d 68 (7th Cir., 1995).

4. For an example of a more recent case—a case that was decided long after the explosion of cell phone usage—that relied on the existence of a cell phone for the finding of probable cause, see *United States v. Fuse*, 391 F.3d 924 (8th Cir. 2004).

5. *United States v. Foreman*, 369 F.3d 776 (4th Cir. 2004).

6. *United States v. Ozbirn*, 189 F.3d 1194 (10th Cir. 1999).

7. Is it the physical presence of the air freshener dangling from the mirror, or the scent of an air freshener, even if sprayed somewhere in the car, that gives rise to probable cause? The answer is both. Or, more precisely, either. For an example of a dangling air freshener, see the case of *United States v. Foreman*, 369 F.3d 776 (4th Cir. 2004). For an example of the scent of air freshener, see the case of *United States v. Patterson*, 65 F.3d 68 (7th Cir. 1995).

8. *United States v. Fuse*, 391 F.3d 924 (8th Cir. 2004).

9. For an example where having a bottle of NoDoz in the car was a factor in the probable cause determination, see ibid.

10. *United States v. Ozbirn*, 189 F.3d 1194 (10th Cir. 1999).

14

1. Danielle E. Chojnacki, Michael D. Cicchini, and Lawrence T. White, *An Empirical Basis for the Admission of Expert Testimony on False Confessions*, 40 ARIZONA STATE LAW JOURNAL 1, 31 (2008), http://www .cicchinilaw.com/Publications.htm (accessed December 28, 2008).

2. Ibid.

3. http://www.fox.com/programming/shows/new/lie_to_me.htm (accessed December 27, 2008).

4. Ibid.

5. Saul M. Kassin and Christina T. Fong, *"I'm Innocent!": Effects of Training on Judgments of Truth and Deception in the Interrogation Room*, 23 LAW & HUMAN BEHAVIOR 499 (1999). An abstract and purchase information available at http://www.springerlink.com/content/l2l57304941075 gp/ (accessed December 27, 2008).

6. Ibid.

7. Ibid.

8. Christian A. Meissner and Saul M. Kassin, *"He's Guilty!": Investigator Bias in Judgments of Truth and Deception*, 26 LAW & HUMAN BEHAVIOR 469 (2002). An abstract and purchase information available at http://www.springerlink.com/content/m0072155k548p528/ (accessed December 27, 2008).

9. Ibid.

10. This hypothetical situation is loosely based on the case of *Green v. Scully*, 850 f.2d 894 (2nd Cir. 1988), where the police stated to the defendant, "I know you did it. I know you did it, Robert. I know you did it." The jury was allowed to hear this recorded interrogation, and the defendant was convicted despite his claims of innocence.

11. For an example of the prohibition on witnesses testifying about the truthfulness of other witnesses, see the case of *State v. Haseltine*, 352 N.W.2d 673 (Wis. Ct. App. 1984).

12. A defendant's statements are considered admissions of a party opponent, an exception to the hearsay rule, and therefore could be used by the state, but usually not by the defendant, at the defendant's criminal trial.

13. This hypothetical situation is based on the case of *Vent v. State*, 67 P.3d 661 (Alaska Ct. App. 2003).

14. Ibid.

15

1. The case law draws a distinction between lying to suspects and fabricating evidence against them, which is called deceit or trickery and is completely legal, and making threats or promises, which generally is considered to be illegal. See, for example, the cases of *United States v. Kontny*,

238 F.3d 815 (7th Cir. 2001) and *United States v. Ceballos*, 302 F.3d 679 (7th Cir. 2002).

2. For a more detailed discussion of the types of interrogation tactics that are used by police, see Danielle E. Chojnacki, Michael D. Cicchini, and Lawrence T. White, *An Empirical Basis for the Admission of Expert Testimony on False Confessions*, 40 ARIZONA STATE LAW JOURNAL 1 (2008), available at http://www.cicchinilaw.com/Publications.htm (accessed December 28, 2008).

3. Ibid., see section III.B.2. for a discussion of the dispositional factors most closely related to false confessions.

4. Ibid., section V.B., table 4.

5. See the Innocence Project, "Understand the Causes: False Confessions," http://www.innocenceproject.org/understand/False-Confessions .php (accessed December 28, 2008).

16

1. *Welsh v. Wisconsin*, 466 U.S. 740 (1984) (internal citations and quotations omitted) (emphasis added).

2. *Johnson v. United States*, 333 U.S. 10 (1948) (emphasis added).

3. For an example of an unknowing and unintelligent yet legally valid waiver of rights, see the case of *Schneckloth v. Bustamante*, 412 U.S. 218 (1973).

4. For an example of a legally valid implied consent, see the case of *United States v. Patten*, 183 F.3d 1190 (10th Cir. 1999).

5. For an example of a legally valid third-party consent, see the case of *United States v. Thomas*, 120 F.3d 564 (5th Cir. 1997).

6. For an example of the police using the hot pursuit doctrine to gain warrantless access to a home, see the case of *United States v. Soto-Beniquez*, 356 F.3d 1 (1st Cir. 2003).

7. For an example of the police employing the exigent circumstance exception, in arguably a nonemergency situation, see the case of *Alvarez v. Montgomery Cty.*, 147 F.3d 354 (4th Cir. 1998).

8. For a case involving the risk of the destruction of evidence, see *United States v. Cephas*, 254 F.3d 388 (4th Cir. 2001); for the risk of flight, see *United States v. Gurdils*, 982 F.2d 64 (2nd Cir. 1992).

9. For an example of the police employing the protective sweep doctrine, see the case of *United States v. Lawlor*, 406 F.3d 37 (1st Cir. 2005).

10. For an example of the police relying on the search incident to

arrest exception, see the case of *United States v. Hernandez*, 941 F.2d 133 (2nd Cir. 1991).

11. For an example of the police relying on the plain sight doctrine, see the case of *Coolidge v. New Hampshire*, 403 U.S. 443 (1971).

17

1. See, for example, the case of *State v. Hutchinson*, 690 N.W.2d 886 (Wis. 2004), which permits a citizen's arrest for even a misdemeanor if it involves a "breach of the peace."

2. See, for example, the case of *United States v. Hillsman et al.*, 522 F.2d 454 (7th Cir. 1975), which discusses the variations on Indiana's citizen's arrest law.

3. "Making a Citizen's Arrest," http://www.allsands.com/howto/citizensarrest_wsg_gn.htm (accessed November 15, 2008).

4. "How to Make a Citizen's Arrest in California," http://www.ehow.com/how_4505960_make-citizens-arrest-california.html (accessed November 15, 2008).

5. "How to Make a Citizen's Arrest," http://www.wikihow.com/Make-a-Citizen%27s-Arrest (accessed November 15, 2008).

6. Ibid.

7. Ibid.

8. Ibid.

9. Ibid.

10. Ibid.

11. "What Is the Law on Citizen's Arrest?" http://www.answerbag.com/q_view/500712 (accessed November 15, 2008).

18

1. U.S. Const. Amend VIII.

2. The strength of the state's allegations, or of the evidence supporting them, is not an important factor when setting bond, as issues of guilt and innocence are reserved for the trial phase of the criminal process. See, for example, the case of *United States v. Gebro*, 948 F.2d 1118 (9th Cir. 1991).

3. See, for example, the case of *United States v. Salerno*, 481 U.S. 739 (1987).

4. See, for example, the case of *Galen v. County of Los Angeles*, 477 F.3d 652 (9th Cir. 2007), where the setting of bail took into account the community's interest in protecting victims of domestic violence.

5. These factors will largely be consistent from state to state, and even from federal district to federal district. The particular factors discussed in this section can be found, for example, in section 969.01 (4) of the Criminal Code of the State of Wisconsin, http://www.legis.state.wi.us/statutes/Stat0969.pdf (accessed December 22, 2008).

6. See ibid., which states that "[i]f bail is imposed, it shall be only in the amount found necessary to assure the appearance of the defendant."

19

1. For a generalized explanation of a waiver process, see "Juvenile 'Waiver' (Transfer to Adult Court)," http://criminal.findlaw.com/crimes/juvenile-justice/juvenile-waiver.html (accessed November 23, 2008).

2. For an example of how a court decides whether to waive a juvenile to adult court, as well as the factors that it may consider, see the case of *J.A.L.*, 471 N.W.2d 493 (Wis. 1991).

3. For an example, see the case of *State v. Avery*, 259 N.W.2d 63 (Wis. 1977).

4. This factual scenario is very common in juvenile and criminal law. For an example, see the case *State v. LeQue*, 442 N.W.2d 494 (Wis. Ct. App. 1989), where a very young defendant was charged in criminal court with sexual assault for an act that allegedly occurred several years earlier when he was a juvenile. The allegation was not made until many years *after* the alleged incident. If the allegation had been made promptly, or even if it had been made a mere twenty days earlier than it was, the defendant would have been in juvenile court. Despite this, his prosecution as an adult was held to be legally proper.

5. See section 938.02(1) of the Criminal Code of the State of Wisconsin, which defines an adult for criminal law purposes as anyone who is seventeen years old or older, http://www.legis.state.wi.us/statutes/Stat0938.pdf (accessed November 23, 2008).

6. For an example of a state law defining domestic abuse or domestic violence, see Section 813.12(am) of the Criminal Code of the State of Wisconsin, http://www.legis.state.wi.us/statutes/Stat0813.pdf (accessed November 23, 2008).

20

1. For proof, look at the caption of any criminal case. If the prosecuting party is the federal government, it will usually read *United States v. Defendant*. If it is one of our state governments, it will usually read *State v. Defendant*, *People v. Defendant*, or *Commonwealth v. Defendant*. In some cases the caption may name two individuals as parties, but one is likely a state warden whom the defendant is suing in a habeas or related action for his release from custody based on a constitutionally defective conviction or sentence.

2. Interestingly, in some cases there can be simultaneous and identically named lawsuits, one criminal and one civil. For example, if you were to punch your neighbor in an argument, you could be sued by your neighbor for civil battery and charged by the state for criminal battery. In that case, your neighbor could dismiss the civil battery case, if he chose to do so, but not the criminal battery case, which lies in the hands of the state.

3. The term "mandatory arrest state" refers to states where the statutes remove or limit the exercise of discretion by police and instead require an arrest of one party whenever a domestic abuse–related accusation is made, even where there is no physical injury. For an example, see the lengthy statutory scheme in section 968.075 of the Criminal Code of the State of Wisconsin, http://www.legis.state.wi.us/statutes/Stat0968.pdf (accessed April 12, 2009).

4. For an example of an obstructing an officer statute, see section 946.41 of the Criminal Code of the State of Wisconsin, http://www.legis .state.wi.us/statutes/Stat0946.pdf (accessed April 12, 2009).

5. For an example of a perjury statute, see section 946.31 of the Criminal Code of the State of Wisconsin, http://www.legis.state.wi.us/statutes/Stat0946.pdf (accessed April 12, 2009).

6. Prior inconsistent statements can be used for impeachment purposes in court and are not considered hearsay. For an example, see section 908.01(4)(a) of the Rules of Evidence of the State of Wisconsin, which mirror the Federal Rules of Evidence, http://www.legis.state.wi.us/statutes/Stat0908.pdf (accessed April 12, 2009).

21

1. This language is modified from section 941.235 of the Criminal Code of the State of Wisconsin, http://www.legis.state.wi.us/statutes/Stat0941.pdf (accessed March 7, 2009).

2. This language is modified from section 947.01 of the Criminal Code of the State of Wisconsin, http://www.legis.state.wi.us/statutes/Stat0947.pdf (accessed March 7, 2009).

3. For example, see section 939.63 of the Criminal Code of the State of Wisconsin, http://www.legis.state.wi.us/statutes/Stat0939.pdf (accessed March 7, 2009), which makes the use of a dangerous weapon a "penalty enhancer."

4. For example, see section 939.22 (10) of the Criminal Code of the State of Wisconsin, http://www.legis.state.wi.us/statutes/Stat0939.pdf (accessed March 7, 2009), which defines "dangerous weapon" to include "any other device or instrumentality which, in the manner it is used or intended to be used, is calculated or likely to produce death or great bodily harm."

5. For example, see the case of *State v. Frey*, 505 N.W.2d 786 (Wis. Ct. App. 1993), where a pillow qualified as a dangerous weapon because it was allegedly used to attempt to suffocate a person.

6. The states of North Carolina, South Carolina, Minnesota, Colorado, Rhode Island, Georgia, Texas, and Iowa have held, at least at one time and in *some* contexts, that hands or other body parts *can* qualify as dangerous or deadly weapons. Conversely, other states such as Wisconsin, Kentucky, Illinois, New York, Michigan, Missouri, Louisiana, Florida, and Arizona have held, at least at one time and in *some* contexts, that hands or other body parts *cannot* qualify as dangerous or deadly weapons. For a discussion, see the case of *State v. Frey*, 505 N.W.2d 786 (Wis. Ct. App. 1993).

7. Ibid.

8. For additional discussion of the bizarre consequences caused by the labeling of hands as dangerous weapons, see *North Carolina v. Hinton*, http://www.aoc.state.nc.us/www/public/sc/opinions/2007/113-06-1.htm (accessed March 7, 2009).

22

1. Federal Rule of Evidence 801 (c), http://www.law.cornell.edu/rules/fre/rules.htm (accessed November 5, 2008).

2. Federal Rule of Evidence 802, http://www.law.cornell.edu/rules/fre/rules.htm (accessed November 5, 2008).

3. Federal Rule of Evidence 803 (2), http://www.law.cornell.edu/rules/fre/rules.htm (accessed November 5, 2008).

4. Federal Rule of Evidence 803 (1), http://www.law.cornell.edu/rules/fre/rules.htm (accessed November 5, 2008).

5. Federal Rule of Evidence 803 (3), http://www.law.cornell.edu/rules/fre/rules.htm (accessed November 5, 2008).

6. See the Sixth Amendment to the United States Constitution, http://www.law.cornell.edu/constitution/constitution.billofrights.html (accessed November 5, 2008).

7. The primary United States Supreme Court cases interpreting the Confrontation Clause are *Crawford v. Washington*, 541 U.S. 36 (2004), and *Davis v. Washington*, 126 S. Ct. 2266 (2006).

8. For an in-depth discussion on how easily prosecutors and courts can bypass the Confrontation Clause, see Michael D. Cicchini, *Judicial (In)Discretion: How Courts Circumvent the Confrontation Clause under Crawford and Davis*, 75 TENNESSEE LAW REVIEW 753 (2009), available at http://cicchinilaw.com/Publications.htm (accessed July 1, 2009).

23

1. See the Sixth Amendment to the United States Constitution, http://www.law.cornell.edu/constitution/constitution.billofrights.html (accessed November 9, 2008).

2. For the four-factor balancing test discussed in this chapter, see the case of *Barker v. Wingo*, 407 U.S. 514 (1972).

3. Ibid.

4. For example, in the case of *United States v. Schreane*, 331 F.3d 548 (6th Cir. 2003), the court held that a delay of nearly fourteen months was not "shockingly long."

5. For an example of this distinction and how the court will use it to find that there was no speedy trial right violation, see the case of *Barker v. Wingo*, 407 U.S. 514 (1972), where the court distinguished between

intentional delays and negligent delays, as well as delays due to court congestion.

6. In fact, both the "frequency and force" of the demands should be considered, according to the court in *Barker*, ibid.

7. In fact, according to the court in the case of *Hakeem v. Beyer*, 990 F.2d 750 (3rd Cir. 1992), even actual incarceration for nearly fifteen months was not sufficient to show prejudice, absent some sort of unusual oppression.

8. For example, see the case of *United States v. Brown*, 325 F.3d 1032 (8th Cir. 2003), where a *three-year delay* was tolerated because the defendant didn't adequately demand the speedy trial. As another example, see the case of *United States v. Tannehill*, 49 F.3d 1049 (5th Cir. 1995), where a *five-and-one-half-year delay* was tolerated because the defendant couldn't show sufficient prejudice to satisfy the court.

24

1. This language is loosely based on the Uniform Controlled Substances Act, adopted by section 961.41 of the Criminal Code of the State of Wisconsin, http://www.legis.state.wi.us/statutes/Stat0961.pdf (accessed February 21, 2009). Although not always explicitly stated in the statute itself, case law often adds an additional requirement that the defendant's possession be knowing possession.

2. This language is loosely based on section 940.225 of the Criminal Code of the State of Wisconsin, http://www.legis.state.wi.us/statutes/Stat0940.pdf (accessed February 21, 2009).

3. This language is loosely based on sections 943.14 and 939.43 of the Criminal Code of the State of Wisconsin, http://www.legis.state.wi.us/statutes/Stat0943.pdf and http://www.legis.state.wi.us/statutes/Stat0939.pdf (accessed February 21, 2009).

4. This language is loosely based on sections 948.09 and 939.43 of the Criminal Code of the State of Wisconsin, http://www.legis.state.wi.us/statutes/Stat0948.pdf and http://www.legis.state.wi.us/statutes/Stat0939.pdf (accessed February 21, 2009).

5. See, for example, section 940.19 of the Criminal Code of the State of Wisconsin, http://www.legis.state.wi.us/statutes/Stat0940.pdf (accessed February 21, 2009).

6. See, for example, section 943.01 of the Criminal Code of the State

of Wisconsin, http://www.legis.state.wi.us/statutes/Stat0943.pdf (accessed February 21, 2009).

7. For example, the crime of reckless child abuse, a version of which can be found in section 948.03 of the Criminal Code of the State of Wisconsin, http://www.legis.state.wi.us/statutes/Stat0948.pdf (accessed February 21, 2009), criminalizes both intentional and reckless conduct that causes any level of harm to a person under eighteen years of age. This includes pain caused from child discipline such as spanking. This statute can, of course, greatly swing the balance of power in the family relationship from the parent to the child, especially in light of mandatory reporters, i.e., those who must report any suspected "child abuse." In these cases, however, the parent may be able to defend the criminal allegation on the basis that the discipline or punishment imposed was reasonable.

8. For example, the crime of negligent injury, a version of which can be found in section 940.24 of the Criminal Code of the State of Wisconsin, http://www.legis.state.wi.us/statutes/Stat0940.pdf (accessed February 21, 2009), criminalizes negligent handling of fire, among other things, no matter how mild or minimal the resulting harm.

9. See, for example, section 948.21 of the Criminal Code of the State of Wisconsin, http://www.legis.state.wi.us/statutes/Stat0940.pdf (accessed February 21, 2009), which criminalizes the "failure to take action" in the context of child welfare.

10. Brent Gurney, Howard Shapiro, and Robert Mays, "The Crime of Doing Nothing: Strict Liability for Corporate Officers under the FDCA," *White Collar Crime Reporter* 22, no. 3 (December 2007), http://www.wilmerhale.com/files/Publication/dab9aa91-7332-4a2e-8f64-62538e409439/Presentation/PublicationAttachment/91ffd641-3959-413e-b8fc-645f3fdab733/The%20Crime%20of%20Doing%20Nothing.pdf (accessed February 21, 2009).

25

1. For a common example of a disorderly conduct statute, see section 947.01 of the Criminal Code of the State of Wisconsin, http://www.legis.state.wi.us/statutes/Stat0947.pdf (accessed November 6, 2008).

2. For a common example of a battery statute, see section 940.19 of the Criminal Code of the State of Wisconsin, http://www.legis.state.wi.us/statutes/Stat0940.pdf (accessed November 6, 2008).

3. For a common example of a felony false imprisonment statute, see section 940.30, ibid.

4. See the Fifth Amendment to the United States Constitution, http://www.law.cornell.edu/constitution/constitution.billofrights.html #amendmentv (accessed November 6, 2008).

5. See the case of *Blockburger v. United Sates*, 284 U.S. 284 U.S. 299 (1932), which has come to be known as "the Blockburger test" for double jeopardy.

6. For example, see the case of *State v. Rabe*, 291 N.W.2d 809 (Wis. 1980), which allows multiple prosecutions of the same criminal statute in the same number of counts as there are victims.

7. For a common example of a felony recklessly endangering safety statute, see section 941.30 (2) of the Criminal Code of the State of Wisconsin, http://www.legis.state.wi.us/statutes/Stat0941.pdf (accessed November 6, 2008).

26

1. See, for example, Wisconsin's Criminal Jury Instruction number 103, which defines "evidence" to include "the sworn testimony of witnesses."

2. *State v. Brown*, 750 N.W.2d 519 (Wis. Ct. App. 2008).

3. Ibid.

4. Ibid.

5. See Michael D. Cicchini and Vincent Rust, *Confrontation after Crawford v. Washington: Defining "Testimonial,"* 10 LEWIS & CLARK LAW REVIEW 531 (2006), and Michael D. Cicchini, *Judicial (In)Discretion: How Courts Circumvent the Confrontation Clause under Crawford and Davis,* 75 TENNESSEE LAW REVIEW 753 (2009), both of which are available at http://www.cicchinilaw.com/Publications.htm (accessed July 1, 2009).

6. See, for example, the case of *State v. Camarena*, 145 P.3d 267, 269 (Ore. Ct. App. 2006).

7. See, for example, the case of *State v. Stahl*, 855 N.E.2d 834, 836 (Ohio 2006).

8. See, for example, the case of *State v. Warsame*, 723 N.W.2d 637, 638 (Minn. Ct. App. 2006).

27

1. For an example of a defendant jumping from a state court system to the federal court system, see the case of *Franklin v. McCaughtry*, 398 F.3d 955 (7th Cir. 2005). There, the defendant was convicted in state court, appealed through the state court system and lost, and then jumped to the federal appellate court. The federal appellate court reversed his state court conviction and ordered a new trial because of a fundamental defect in the state court proceedings.

2. Battery typically does not require any physical injury. Instead, if the alleged victim reports pain or says that he was "hurt," that is sufficient for conviction. For an example of a battery statute, see section 940.19 (1) of the Criminal Code of the State of Wisconsin, http://www.legis.state.wi.us/statutes/Stat0940.pdf (accessed January 24, 2009), which requires only "bodily harm." "Bodily harm," in turn, is defined by section 939.22 (4) to include "physical pain," no matter how slight, http://www.legis.state.wi.us/statutes/Stat0939.pdf (accessed January 24, 2009).

3. For a horrifying example of a defendant being convicted and sentenced to many years in prison, based on an implausible allegation by an alleged victim who admitted to be *sleeping* during the time of the alleged crime, and with no other evidence whatsoever, see the case of *State v. Brown*, 750 N.W.2d 519 (Wis. Ct. App. 2008).

4. Generally speaking, the defendant must be convicted based on what he did or didn't do, not on what his character is, what he has a tendency to do, or what he has done in the past. For an example, see section 904.04 of the Evidence Code of the State of Wisconsin, http://www.legis.state.wi.us/statutes/Stat0904.pdf (accessed January 24, 2009).

5. Prior specific instances of untruthful conduct, such as committing perjury, are admissible because they call into question the truthfulness of the witness who is testifying. For an example, see section 906.08 (2) of the Evidence Code of the State of Wisconsin, http://www.legis.state.wi.us/statutes/Stat0906.pdf (accessed January 24, 2009).

6. Under *Brady v. Maryland*, 373 U.S. 83 (1963), prosecutors have a legal duty to turn over exculpatory evidence.

7. For an article discussing various methods by which prosecutors commit misconduct in closing arguments, see Michael D. Cicchini, *Prosecutorial Misconduct at Trial: A New Perspective Rooted in Confrontation Clause Jurisprudence*, 37 Seton Hall Law Review 335 (2007), available at www.cicchinilaw.com.

8. The Sixth Amendment to the United States Constitution guarantees that everyone charged with a crime receives the effective assistance of counsel. However, the term "effective" does not mean error free.

9. For an excellent example of the "harmless error" doctrine in action, see the case of *State v. Mayo*, 734 N.W.2d 115 (Wis. 2007), where "[t]he prosecutor's improper conduct was exacerbated by the defense counsel's deficient performance in failing to investigate, in failing to present a corroborating witness, in failing to procure the testimony of the complaining witness at the preliminary examination to use for impeachment purposes, and in failing to object when the prosecutor erred." Nonetheless, the jury's guilty verdict was upheld and the defendant was denied his request for a new trial.

10. Even in cases of obvious and intentional prosecutorial misconduct, prosecutors will nearly always get a second chance at a conviction. In other words, the defendant's remedy is not dismissal of his case but rather a retrial and a fresh start for the prosecutor. See *Oregon v. Kennedy*, 456 U.S. 667 (1982); Cicchini, *Prosecutorial Misconduct at Trial*, 335, 356–57.

11. For an example of an increased punishment at resentencing, see the case of *State v. Naydihor*, 678 N.W.2d 220 (Wis. 2004).

28

1. Toni Locy, "Supreme Court Upholds Arizona Sanity Law," June 30, 2006, http://www.law.com/jsp/law/LawArticleFriendly.jsp?id=11515719 21058 (accessed December 24, 2008).

2. This language is a paraphrase of the definition of competency as found in section 971.13 of the Criminal Code of the State of Wisconsin, http://www.legis.state.wi.us/statutes/Stat0971.pdf (accessed December 24, 2008).

3. See, for example, section 971.14 of the Criminal Code of the State of Wisconsin, http://www.legis.state.wi.us/statutes/Stat0971.pdf (accessed December 24, 2008).

4. See, for example, ibid.

5. See, for example, Locy, "Supreme Court Upholds Arizona Sanity Law."

6. See, for example, section 971.16 of the Criminal Code of the State of Wisconsin, http://www.legis.state.wi.us/statutes/Stat0971.pdf (accessed December 24, 2008).

7. See, for example, Locy, "Supreme Court Upholds Arizona Sanity Law."

8. See, for example, section 971.17 of the Criminal Code of the State of Wisconsin, http://www.legis.state.wi.us/statutes/Stat0971.pdf (accessed December 24, 2008).

29

1. For examples of how prosecutors and judges are able to bypass a defendant's right of confrontation, see Michael D. Cicchini, *Judicial (In)Discretion: How Courts Circumvent the Confrontation Clause under Crawford and Davis*, 75 TENNESSEE LAW REVIEW 753 (2009), http://cicchinilaw.com/Publications.htm (accessed April 12, 2009).

2. See the case of *Godinez v. Moran*, 113 S. Ct. 2680 (1993).

3. For a discussion of competence to stand trial, see the case of *State v. Byrge*, 614 N.W.2d 477 (Wis. 2000).

4. For an example of a competency evaluation procedure, see section 971.14 of the Criminal Code of the State of Wisconsin, http://www.legis.state.wi.us/statutes/Stat0971.pdf (accessed April 12, 2009).

5. For an example of this waiver colloquy, see the case of *State v. Coleman*, 644 N.W.2d 383 (Wis. Ct. App. 2002).

6. For an example of a case imposing a higher level of competency before a defendant may proceed *pro se*, see *State v. Klessig*, 564 N.W.2d 716 (Wis. 1997).

7. For a discussion of a trial court's use of standby counsel, see the case of *Faretta v. California*, 422 U.S. 806 (1975).

30

1. Internet Movie Database, *Wild Things*, http://www.imdb.com/title/tt0120890/ (accessed November 5, 2008).

2. Drew's Script-O-Rama, *Wild Things* script, http://www.script-o-rama.com/movie_scripts/w/wild-things-script-transcript-denise.html (accessed November 5, 2008).

3. For example, see the State of Wisconsin's Office of the State Public Defender, http://www.wisspd.org/ (accessed November 5, 2008).

4. See *Gideon v. Wainwright*, 372 U.S. 335 (1963), which discusses the scope of the Sixth Amendment right to counsel in criminal cases.

5. For example, see the American Counsel of Chief Defenders Statement on Caseloads and Workloads, http://dpa.ky.gov/news/2008/Item%2027%20ACCD%20Statement%20on%20Caseloads.pdf (accessed November 5, 2008).

6. "Citing Workload, Public Lawyers Reject New Cases," *New York Times*, http://www.nytimes.com/2008/11/09/us/09defender.html (accessed November 9, 2008).

7. For example, see Morris B. Hoffman, Paul H. Rubin, and Joanna M. Sheppard, *An Empirical Study of Public Defender Effectiveness: Self-Selection by the "Marginally Indigent,"* 3 OHIO STATE JOURNAL OF CRIMINAL LAW 223 (2005), wherein the authors suggest that some public defender clients, "by self-selection, tend to have less defensible cases." In other words, if a person who qualifies for public defender representation has a strong case, that person may be more motivated to somehow obtain the funds to hire a private attorney, thereby helping to fulfill the prophecy that private attorneys get better outcomes than public defenders. In this case, however, it would be due to having stronger cases to begin with, not from rendering better legal services. See http://moritzlaw.osu.edu/osjcl/Articles/Volume3_1/Commentary/Hoffman_3-1.pdf (accessed November 5, 2008).

8. When a person is charged with a crime, the judge or commissioner may set a high-cash bail to, in theory, assure the person's appearance in court. For example, see Chapter 969 of the Criminal Code of the State of Wisconsin, http://www.legis.state.wi.us/statutes/Stat0969.pdf (accessed November 5, 2008). In reality, however, cash bail is often set at a high level for other improper reasons and results in lengthy pretrial detention for indigent defendants.

9. For example, the Office of the Wisconsin State Public Defender has an Assigned Counsel Division that provides support to private attorneys who take appointed cases, at a reduced fee, from the state public defender. See http://www.wisspd.org/html/acd/acd.asp (accessed November 5, 2008).

31

1. *Gideon v. Wainwright*, 372 U.S. 335 (1963).

2. "Indigency Law and Legal Definition," uslegal.com, http://definitions.uslegal.com/i/indigency/ (accessed January 23, 2009).

3. Ibid.

4. "Obtaining a Criminal Defense Lawyer," findlaw.com, http://criminal.findlaw.com/crimes/criminal_help/obtaining-a-criminal-defense-lawyer.html (accessed January 24, 2009).

5. Ibid.

6. Ibid.

7. Laura Miranda, "Ask a Lawyer Archive," lawyers.com, http://criminal-law.lawyers.com/ask-a-lawyer/Indigency-Hearing-6323.html (accessed January 24, 2009).

8. "Frequently Asked Questions," North Carolina Court System, http://www.nccourts.org/Support/FAQs/FAQs.asp?Type=2&language=1#8 4 (accessed January 23, 2009).

9. Sometimes, however, various legal aid clinics may be able to provide citizens with representation, or at least assistance, on such civil matters.

10. While the Constitution guarantees the assistance of counsel, it does not necessarily guarantee the assistance of a defendant's counsel of choice.

11. "Before You Fire Your Court Appointed Lawyer," lawyers.com, http://research.lawyers.com/Before-You-Fire-Your-Court-Appointed-Lawyer.html (accessed January 24, 2009).

12. In one instance known to this author, a woman whose own sister accused her of misdemeanor battery did just this, and did so on the advice of the very police officer who arrested her, who told her that she wouldn't need a lawyer on such a "minor" charge.

13. "What You Don't Know Can Hurt You," fairdefense.org, http://fairdefense.org/why_lawyer.pdf (accessed January 23, 2009).

32

1. See Joseph M. Perillo, *Calamari and Perillo on Contracts* § 19.1 (a) (5th ed. 2003).

2. See ibid. at § 1.1.

3. See ibid., ch. 2.

4. See ibid., ch. 4.

5. See ibid., §§ 19.1–19.25.

33

1. For a more detailed discussion of illegality, public policy, and enforceability, see the Restatement (Second) of Contracts, section 178.

2. For an example of a zoning law case, see the case of *McMahon v. Anderson et al.*, 728 A.2d 656 (D.C. App. 1999). In fact, while the term "illegal" seems quite ominous, well-meaning parties may not even know that their contracts are illegal, and in some cases, the law they violate may not even be a criminal law or even a statute of any kind. An excellent example of this is a contingent fee in a criminal case, which is illegal, and therefore unenforceable, because it violates the attorney's rules of professional conduct.

3. For example, in late 2008, the governor of Illinois was accused of agreeing to sell the US Senate seat previously occupied by President-Elect Barack Obama, a contract that, *if proved to exist*, would clearly be void as against public policy, and potentially criminal. See Jeff Coen and Rick Pearson, "Blagojevich Arrested on Federal Charges," chicagobreaking news.com, http://www.chicagobreakingnews.com/2008/12/source-feds -take-gov-blagojevich-into-custody.html (accessed January 11, 2009).

4. For an example of a fraud defense in a contract case, see *Gregory v. Chemical Waste Management*, 38 F.Supp. 2d 598 (W.D. Tenn. 1996).

5. For a discussion of legal impossibility and the related doctrine of impracticability, see the case of *Transatlantic Financing v. U.S.*, 363 F.2d 312 (D.C. cir. 1966).

34

1. For the definition, history, evolution, and examples of promissory estoppel, see Joseph M. Perillo, *Calamari and Perillo on Contracts*, ch. 6 (5th ed. 2003).

35

1. "Bart Sells His Soul," Wikipedia, http://en.wikipedia.org/wiki/Bart _Sells_His_Soul (accessed November 5, 2008).

2. See ch. 32 for a discussion of what constitutes an enforceable contract.

3. Joseph M. Perillo, *Calamari and Perillo on Contracts* § 8.1 (5th ed. 2003).

4. Ibid. § 8.6 (a).
5. Ibid. § 8.8.
6. Ibid. § 8.6 (b).
7. Ibid. § 8.7 (b).
8. Ibid. § 8.4 (a).
9. Ibid. § 8.6 (a).

36

1. This exculpatory clause is taken from the case of *Atkins v. Swimwest Family Fitness Ctr.*, 691 N.W.2d 334 (Wis. 2005).

2. See, for example, the case of *Heenan v. Fireman's Funds Ins. Co.*, 616 N.W.2d 923 (Wis. 2000).

3. *Atkins v. Swimwest Family Fitness Ctr.*, 691 N.W.2d 334 (Wis. 2005). For another example of an exculpatory clause that was too vague to be enforceable, see the case of *Dobratz v. Thomson*, 468 N.W.2d 654 (Wis. 1991).

4. See the *Atkins* case, ibid.

5. For an example of a case discussing the bargaining power of the parties, see *Disc. Fabric House v. Wis. Tel. Co.*, 345 N.W.2d 417 (Wis. 1984).

6. For a case discussing the nature of the service being offered and how it relates to the enforceability of the exculpatory clause, see *Merten v. Nathan*, 321 N.W.2d 173 (Wis. 1982).

37

1. Joseph M. Perillo, *Calamari and Perillo on Contracts* § 9.40 (5th ed. 2003) (quoting the case of *Gimbel Bros. v. Swift*, 307 N.Y.S.2d 952 [1970]).

2. Ibid., § 9.38.

3. Ibid., discussing multiple cases and the general factors that courts will often consider in determining what is unconscionable.

4. Ibid. at § 13.12.

5. Ibid.

6. Ibid. at § 14.31.

38

1. *Goldstein v. Rosenthal*, 288 N.Y.S. 2d 503 (Civ. Ct. 1968).

2. *Brown v. Thomas*, 379 N.W.2d 868 (Wis. Ct. App. 1985).

3. *Pavlicic v. Vogtsberger*, 136 A.2d 127 (Pa. 1957).

4. Wisconsin and New York are two such "no-fault" states. For an example of how the no-fault rule was applied, see the case of *Brown v. Thomas*, 379 N.W.2d 868 (Wis. Ct. App. 1985).

5. *Gaden v. Gaden*, 323 N.Y.S.2d 955 (1971).

6. *Wilson v. Dabo*, 461 N.E.2d 8 (Ohio App. 1983).

7. *Brown v. Thomas*, 379 N.W.2d 868 (Wis. Ct. App. 1985).

39

1. Section 767.41 (5) of the Wisconsin statutes, http://www.legis.state.wi.us/statutes/Stat0767.pdf (accessed January 18, 2009).

2. Section 767.41 (2) of the Wisconsin statutes, http://www.legis.state.wi.us/statutes/Stat0767.pdf (accessed January 18, 2009).

3. Section 767.41 (2) (am) of the Wisconsin statutes, http://www.legis.state.wi.us/statutes/Stat0767.pdf (accessed January 18, 2009).

4. The examples used in this paragraph are derived from sections 767.41 (2) (b) and (d) of the Wisconsin statutes, http://www.legis.state.wi.us/statutes/Stat0767.pdf (accessed January 18, 2009).

5. Section 767.41 (5) of the Wisconsin statutes, http://www.legis.state.wi.us/statutes/Stat0767.pdf (accessed January 18, 2009).

6. The examples used in the numbered paragraphs are derived from sections 767.41 (4) and (5) of the Wisconsin statutes, http://www.legis.state.wi.us/statutes/Stat0767.pdf (accessed January 18, 2009).

40

1. For example, see Huggins Law Office, http://www.hugginslawfirm.com/PracticeAreas/Premarital-Agreements.asp ("A premarital agreement might not seem important now, but it could help alleviate serious problems down the road if the marriage does not work out") (accessed January 18, 2009).

2. For an example of a divorced couple fighting over the enforceability of a pre-nup, see the case of *Weissgerber v. Weissgerber*, 686 N.W.2d 455

(Wis. Ct. App. 2004). This case also discusses and applies the legal test that has been described in this chapter.

3. *Button v. Button*, 388 N.W.2d 546 (Wis. 1986).

4. An excellent example of a party's efforts increasing asset value, thereby voiding the original pre-nup for unfairness, is *Krejci v. Krejci*, 667 N.W.2d 780 (Wis. Ct. App. 2003).

41

1. For example, see section 948.22 of the Criminal Code of the State of Wisconsin, which criminalizes the failure to pay child support. If the person fails to pay for 120 days or more, the crime is a felony for which the person could be sent to prison. See http://www.legis.state.wi.us/statutes/Stat0948.pdf (accessed November 5, 2008).

2. This language is an abbreviated version of section 891.41 of the Wisconsin statutes, which explains the different ways in which a man will be presumed to be a child's father. See http://www.legis.state.wi.us/statutes/Stat0891.pdf (accessed November 5, 2008).

3. For example, see the case of *State v. Bogart*, 552 N.W.2d 898 (Wis. Ct. App. 1996), where Mr. Bogart claimed that the children whom he was ordered to support were not his own. However, his mere allegation that his wife was "adulterous," without specific details about her adulterous behavior, was insufficient to convince the court to order DNA tests so that Bogart could prove he was not the father.

4. For example, see the case of *Randy A.J. v. Norma I.J.*, 677 N.W.2d 630 (Wis. 2004).

42

1. Internal Revenue Service, Publication 525: Taxable and Nontaxable Income: Miscellaneous Income: Other Income: Found Property (2008) at 33, http://www.irs.gov/pub/irs-pdf/p525.pdf (accessed January 17, 2009).

2. Section 61(1), Title 26, United States Code Annotated (emphasis added).

3. The facts used in this book are adapted from the case of *Cesarini v. United States*, 296 F.Supp. 3 (N.D. Ohio, 1969), affirmed at 428 F.2d 812 (6th Cir. 1970).

4. Ibid. (citing a relevant treasury regulation that interprets the language of the tax code).

5. Ibid. (discussing the various laws regarding legal rights of finders of treasure-troves).

6. Ibid.

7. "The Big Catch Could Have a Big Catch," *Wall Street Journal* Tax Report, July 25, 2007, http://online.wsj.com/article/SB118532191532076 935.html (accessed January 17, 2009).

8. Ibid. Interestingly, of those who believe the ball would be taxable income the moment it is caught, some don't think the IRS would actually make the owner of the ball pay taxes until it is sold, for fear of being viewed as a politically unpopular bully.

9. Ibid.

43

1. Internal Revenue Service, "Bartering," http://www.irs.gov/businesses/small/article/0,,id=187920,00.html (accessed January 17, 2009).

2. Internal Revenue Service, Publication 525: Taxable and Nontaxable Income: Miscellaneous Income: Bartering (2008) at 19, http://www.irs.gov/pub/irs-pdf/p525.pdf (accessed January 17, 2009).

3. That's not to say that just because something is complex, or even mind-bogglingly complex, that it will be legal. For example, many highly complex tax shelters, even some of those developed by reputable accounts and lawyers, have been found to be nothing more than hollow scams designed to avoid paying taxes, and therefore illegal.

4. Internal Revenue Service, Publication 525: Taxable and Nontaxable Income: Miscellaneous Income: Bartering (2008) at 19, http://www.irs.gov/pub/irs-pdf/p525.pdf (accessed January 17, 2009).

5. Ibid.

6. Ibid.

44

1. "New York Enacts Changes to Adverse Possession Law to Require Claim of Right," http://lawoftheland.wordpress.com/2008/07/11/new -york-enacts-changes-to-adverse-possession-law-to-require-claim-of-right/ (accessed February 6, 2009).

2. See, for example, Konstantine Kyros, "Adverse Possession: Basics," http://www.lawyerviews.com/lawsite/basicinfo/ap.html, and Aaron Larson, "Adverse Possession," http://www.expertlaw.com/library/real_estate/ adverse_possession.html (accessed February 6, 2009), and the case of *Pierz v. Gorski*, 276 N.W.2d 352 (Wis. Ct. App. 1979) (requiring use that is "open, notorious, visible, exclusive, hostile and continuous" in order to make a claim of adverse possession).

3. Ibid.

4. Ibid.

5. Ibid.

6. Ibid.

7. Ibid.

8. "New York Enacts Changes to Adverse Possession Law to Require Claim of Right."

45

1. Jesse S. Ishikawa, *Wisconsin Law of Easements*, ch. 1, p. 2 (3rd ed., 2007).

2. For an example of an easement document, see ibid., App. C.

3. Ibid., App. C, p. 4.

4. Ibid., ch. 2, p. 9 (discussing *McCormick v. Schubring*, 672 N.W.2d 63 [Wis. 2003]).

5. Ibid., ch. 2, p. 14.

46

1. "Negligence," Wikipedia, http://en.wikipedia.org/wiki/Negligence (accessed March 1, 2009).

2. "The Actual Facts about the McDonald's Coffee Case," http://www .lectlaw.com/files/cur78.htm (accessed March 1, 2009).

3. Ibid.

4. Ibid.

5. O'Brien, Shafner, Stuart, Kelly & Morris, P.C., "The McDonald's Coffee Cup Case: Separating the McFacts from the McFiction," http:// library.findlaw.com/1999/Nov/1/129862.html (accessed March 1, 2009).

6. Andrea Gerlin, "McDonald's Coffee Lawsuit: McDonald's Callous-

ness Was Real Issue, Jurors Say, in Case of Burned Woman," *Wall Street Journal*, September 1, 1994, available at http://www.vanfirm.com/mcdonalds-coffee-lawsuit.htm (accessed March 1, 2009).

7. Ibid.

8. O'Brien, Shafner, Stuart, Kelly & Morris, P.C., "The McDonald's Coffee Cup Case."

9. Gerlin, "McDonald's Coffee Lawsuit."

10. Ibid.

11. Rebecca McGeehan, "Tort Reform in the McDonald's Coffee Burn Case," *Associated Content*, September 19, 2008, http://www.associatedcontent.com/article/1021670/tort_reform_in_the_mcdonalds_coffee.html?cat=17 (accessed March 1, 2009).

12. Ibid.

47

1. For a discussion of the duty of care to trespassers, see, for example, *Lockwood v. Bowman Const. Co.*, 101 F.3d 1231 (7th Cir. 1996).

2. Ted Frank, "The Burglar and the Skylight: Another Debunking That Isn't," Overlawyered: Chronicling the High Cost of Our Legal System, September 25, 2006, http://overlawyered.com/2006/09/the-burglar-and-the-skylight-another-debunking-that-isnt/ (accessed March 22, 2009).

3. Wendy Lilliedoll, "An Unexpected Windfall for California's Tort Reform Movement: *Bodine v. Enterprise High School*," http://74.125.93.104/search?q=cache:07WgroZZk-MJ:www.law.berkeley.edu/faculty/sugarmans/Wendy%2520TortStoryFinal%2520ii.doc+bodine+v+enterprise&cd=1&hl=en&ct=clnk&gl=us&client=firefox-a (accessed March 29, 2009).

4. Frank, "The Burglar and the Skylight."

5. Ibid.

6. Shannon P. Duffy, "17-Year-Old Trespassers May Use Attractive Nuisance Argument," *Legal Intelligencer*, April 11, 2006, http://www.law.com/jsp/article.jsp?id=1144672792491 (accessed March 22, 2009).

7. Ibid.

8. US District Judge Lawrence F. Stengel, as quoted in Duffy, "17-Year-Old Trespassers May Use Attractive Nuisance Argument."

9. For a discussion of the typical elements of the attractive nuisance

doctrine, see the case of *Christians v. Homestake Enterprises Ltd.*, 303 N.W.2d 608 (Wis. 1981).

10. Duffy, "17-Year-Old Trespassers May Use Attractive Nuisance Argument."

11. *Katko v. Briney*, 183 N.W.2d 657 (Iowa, 1971).

12. "Accused Burglar Sues Homeowner Who Shot Him," ABC12WISN.com, posted September 27, 2006, http://www.wisn.com/news/9950016/detail.html (accessed March 29, 2009).

13. Ibid.

48

1. For the exact language of Wisconsin's Good Samaritan statute, for example, see the case of *Mueller v. McMillan Warner Ins. Co.*, 714 N.W.2d 183 (Wis. 2006).

2. For a discussion of the duty to rescue and its applicability, see, for example, *Stockberger v. United States*, 332 F.3d 479 (7th Cir. 2003). See also "Good Samaritan Law," Wikipedia, http://en.wikipedia.org/wiki/Good_Samaritan_law (accessed April 11, 2009).

3. Paul Elias, "Suing Your Savior: Court Ruling Leaves Do-Gooders Legally Liable," *Washington News*, December 20, 2008, http://www.nbcwashington.com/news/us_world/Suing-Your-Savior.html?corder=&pg=1 (accessed April 12, 2009).

4. "Good Samaritan Law & Legal Definition," *US Legal: Definitions*, http://definitions.uslegal.com/g/good-samaritans/ (accessed April 11, 2009).

5. Rod Brouhard, "How Much Are You Protected by Good Samaritan Laws?" about.com, September 4, 2007, http://firstaid.about.com/od/medicallegal/qt/goodsam.htm (accessed April 12, 2009).

6. Ibid.

7. "Can You Get Sued for Reviving Someone with CPR?" http://answers.yahoo.com/question/index?qid=20080422194005AAf2J9Q (accessed April 11, 2009).

8. Brouhard, "How Much Are You Protected by Good Samaritan Laws?"

9. "What Is a Good Samaritan Statute?" *Nursing Legal Issues, Medi-Smart: Nursing Education Resources*, http://www.medi-smart.com/gslaw.htm (accessed April 12, 2009).

10. "What Is the Good Samaritan Law?" *Essortment*, http://www.essortment.com/all/goodsamaritanl_redg.htm (accessed April 11, 2009).

11. "Duty to Rescue," Wikipedia, http://en.wikipedia.org/wiki/Duty_to_rescue (accessed April 11, 2009).

12. Ibid.

49

1. "Libel and Slander," *Enotes: Encyclopedia of Everyday Law*, http://www.enotes.com/everyday-law-encyclopedia/libel-and-slander (accessed April 24, 2009).

2. Ibid.

3. "How to Avoid a Defamation of Character Claim," eHow legal editor, http://www.ehow.com/how_2122181_avoid-defamation-character-claim.html (accessed April 24, 2009).

4. "Libel and Slander," *Enotes: Encyclopedia of Everyday Law*.

5. Ibid.

6. "How to Sue for Defamation of Character," eHow legal editor, http://www.ehow.com/how_2063889_sue-defamation-character.html (accessed April 24, 2009).

7. "Libel and Slander Misinformation," dancingwithlawyers.com, http://www.dancingwithlawyers.com/freeinfo/libel-slander-mis-information.shtml (accessed April 24, 2009).

8. J. Craig Williams, "Slander Per Se versus Slander Per Quod," http://www.mayitpleasethecourt.com/journal.asp?blogid=1985 (accessed April 25, 2009).

9. Ibid.

10. "Libel and Slander Misinformation."

11. "How to Sue Someone for Slander," eHow legal editor, http://www.ehow.com/how_2040839_sue-someone-slander.html (accessed April 24, 2009).

12. "Libel and Slander," *Enotes: Encyclopedia of Everyday Law*.

50

1. "Abraham Lincoln," Lawyer Hall of Fame, http://www.fansoffieger.com/lincoln.htm (accessed November 12, 2008).

2. "Trivia for *Young Mr. Lincoln*," http://www.imdb.com/title/tt0032155/trivia (accessed November 12, 2008).

3. "Duke Law Dedicates J. Michael Goodson Law Library," *Duke Law News & Events*, http://www.law.duke.edu/news/story?id=2734&u=11 (accessed November 30, 2008).

4. "ABA Approved Law Schools," *American Bar Association*, http://www.abanet.org/legaled/approvedlawschools/approved.html (accessed November 18, 2008).

5. G. Jeffrey MacDonald, "The Self Made Lawyer," *Christian Science Monitor*, June 3, 2003, http://www.csmonitor.com/2003/0603/p13s01-lecs.html (accessed November 12, 2008).

6. "State Bar of California," http://www.medbib.com/State_Bar_of_California; see also "Rules Regulating Admission to Practice Law in California, the State Bar of California; Title IV: Admissions and Educational Standards," http://calbar.ca.gov/calbar/pdfs/rules/Rules_Title4_Div1-Adm-Prac-Law.pdf (accessed November 12, 2008).

7. James Bandler and Nathan Koppel, "Raising the Bar: Even Top Lawyers Fail California Bar," *Wall Street Journal*, December 5, 2005, A1, reprinted in lawschool.com, http://www.lawschool.com/deanfails.htm (accessed November 30, 2008).

8. Associated Press, "Skipping Law School. Lincoln Did It. Why Not the Valoises?" *New York Times*, September 21, 2005, http://www.nytimes.com/2005/09/21/national/21lawyers.html (accessed November 30, 2008).

9. Eisla Sebastian, "Vermont Bar Exam: A Basic Guide," *Associated Content*, July 11, 2006, http://www.associatedcontent.com/article/42706/vermont_bar_exam_a_basic_guide.html (accessed November 30, 2008).

10. Ibid.

11. "MPRE Review," *MicroMash Bar Review*, http://www.micromashbar.com/wps/portal/micromashbar/barexaminfo/mpre (accessed November 30, 2008).

51

1. Tara Kuther, "What Is the Bar Exam?" about.com, Graduate School, http://gradschool.about.com/od/lawschool/f/barexam.htm (accessed November 29, 2008).

2. Avrum D. Lank, "Legal Group Looks at Dropping Bar Exam," *Milwaukee Journal Sentinel*, September 25, 2006, http://www.lawschool.com/wisconsinmay.htm (accessed November 30, 2008).

3. "Diploma Privilege," Wikipedia, http://en.wikipedia.org/wiki/ Diploma_privilege (accessed December 1, 2008).

4. Patricia Mell, "Crossing the Bar, Not the Primrose Path: Educating Lawyers at the Turn of the Last Century," MICHIGAN BAR JOURNAL 79, no. 7, July 2000, http://www.michbar.org/journal/article.cfm?articleID=99 &volumeID=9 (accessed November 30, 2008).

5. Richard L. Abel, "United States: The Contradictions of Professionalism," *Lawyers in Society: The Common Law World*, ed. Richard L. Abel and Philip S. C. Lewis (Beard Books, 2006), pp. 186–234, http://books .google.com/books?id=2SPiIRFY4_sC&pg=PA195&lpg=PA195&dq=why +states+end+the+diploma+privilege&source=web&ots=ME5LGlDZpv &sig=La9XC0iqOKItfYWsC0OhfCXTf9o&hl=en&sa=X&oi=book _result&resnum=9&ct=result#PPR7,M1 (accessed November 29, 2008).

6. Derrick Nunnally, "State's Law Students Get Free Pass on Bar Exam," *Milwaukee Journal Sentinel*, August 6, 2004, http://www.law school.com/freepass.htm (accessed November 29, 2008).

7. Oliver Rundell, as quoted in "A History of the Organized Bar in Wisconsin: Chapter Thirteen, Admission to the Bar," wisbar.org, http:// www.wisbar.org/AM/Template.cfm?Section=BarHistory&TEMPLATE=/ CM/ContentDisplay.cfm&CONTENTID=48667 (accessed November 29, 2008).

8. Ibid.

9. Lank, "Legal Group Looks at Dropping Bar Exam."

10. Ibid.

11. Plaintiffs-appellants principal brief in *Wiesmueller v. Kosobucki*, http://74.125.45.132/search?q=cache:zmKkpEncSZEJ:law.marquette.edu/cgi -bin/site.pl%3F25%26fileID%3D33139+Wiesmueller+v.+Kosubucki&hl =en&ct=clnk&cd=3&gl=us&client=firefox-a (accessed November 30, 2008).

12. "News 12 Investigates: Not All Wisconsin Lawyers Have Passed Competency Exams," Milwaukee News Channel 12, http://www.wisn .com/video/9582768/index.html (accessed November 29, 2008).

13. Ibid.

14. Lank, "Legal Group Looks at Dropping Bar Exam."

52

1. For a detailed discussion of the plea bargaining process in criminal cases, including citations and statistics regarding the number of cases that

resolve by plea bargain, see Michael D. Cicchini, *Broken Government Promises: A Contract-Based Approach to Enforcing Plea Bargains*, 38 NEW MEXICO LAW REVIEW 159 (2008), http://www.cicchinilaw.com/Publications.htm (accessed December 2, 2008).

2. For examples of the different types of transactional lawyers and practices discussed in this chapter, simply visit the Web sites of some of the major US law firms, including Quarles & Brady LLP, http://quarles.com/Services/ (accessed December 2, 2008).

53

1. "Georgia Law: Financial Information," http://www.law.uga.edu/admissions/jd/financial/index.html#Estimated (accessed November 16, 2008).

2. "Emory Law School: Tuition and Fees," http://www.law.emory.edu/admission/financing-an-emory-law-degree/tuition-and-fees.html (accessed November 16, 2008).

3. "University of Illinois College of Law: Costs/Tuition," http://www.law.uiuc.edu/prospective-students/costs-tuition.asp (accessed November 16, 2008).

4. "Northwestern Law: Tuition and Financial Aid," http://www.law.northwestern.edu/admissions/tuitionaid/tuition.html (accessed November 16, 2008).

5. "Marquette University Law School: Tuition, Financial Aid and Scholarships," http://law.marquette.edu/cgi-bin/site.pl?prospective/tuition (accessed November 16, 2008).

6. *Marquette Lawyer* Online, "Joe Zilber: Another Historic Gift," http://law.marquette.edu/s3/site/images/magazine/springSummer2008.pdf (accessed November 16, 2008).

7. *U.S. News & World Report* Online, "Law: Whose Graduates Have the Most Debt? The Least?" http://grad-schools.usnews.rankingsandreviews.com/grad/law/grad_debt (accessed November 16, 2008).

8. "Law Firm Salary Increases Raise Eyebrows, Expectations," http://www.law.com/jsp/article.jsp?id=1170842573516 (accessed November 16, 2008).

9. "Distribution of 2006 Starting Salaries: Best Graphic Chart of the Year," *Empirical Legal Studies*, http://www.elsblog.org/the_empirical_legal_studi/2007/09/distribution-of.html (accessed November 16, 2008).

Index

adultery, 53–55, 241–42

adverse possession, 195–97, 200, 264–65

attractive nuisance, 208, 266–67

avoidance, 55, 87, 147, 151–52, 154, 156–58, 164, 183, 191, 199, 264, 268

bail, 34–35, 87–89, 137, 248, 258

bail jumping, 34–36, 238

bartering, 190–91, 264

battery, 29–31, 36, 82, 94, 98–99, 110, 113, 116, 122–23, 203, 249, 253, 255, 259

bond, 34–36, 87–89, 109, 237–38, 247

bright-line rule, 109

burglary, 75, 82, 127

child support, 181–83, 263

citizen's arrest, 81–84, 247

competency, 125–26, 130–31

concealed weapons, 41–43, 99

Confrontation Clause, 106, 251, 254, 255, 257

contract, 34, 92–93, 142, 147–49, 150–52, 153–55, 156–59, 160–63, 164–67, 222, 226, 233, 259–61, 271

custody, 36, 70, 126–27, 137, 142–43, 174–76, 226, 238, 243, 249

damages, 110, 151, 165, 167, 203–206, 207, 209, 216

dangerous weapons, 41, 43, 97–100, 250

defamatory statement, 215–16

diploma privilege, 222–24, 270

disclaimer, 160

disorderly conduct, 24–25, 35, 37–40, 43, 92, 97, 116, 122, 126–28, 235, 238–39, 253

divorce, 54–55, 70, 142, 174–75, 177–80, 181–82, 226, 262

DNA test, 182, 263

double jeopardy, 115–17, 254

drunk driving (DUI, DWI, or OWI), 23, 26–28, 79, 236

due process, 18, 51

easement, 198–200, 265

Eighth Amendment, 87

excited utterance, 104

exculpatory clause, 160–63, 261

facts and circumstances, 18, 65–67, 78, 88, 161, 164, 209

false accusation, 70, 82
false imprisonment, 82, 94, 116, 254
Fifth Amendment, 54–55, 254
firearm, 33, 36, 38, 41–43, 49, 97–98, 143
First Amendment, 216
flight risk, 88–89
Fourth Amendment, 77
frustration of purpose, 166–67
full capacity, 156

Good Samaritan, 83, 210–13, 267–68

harmless error doctrine, 123–24, 256
hearsay, 103–106, 119, 245, 249
heart balm actions, 54

incompetency, 126, 215
indigency, 140–41, 258–59
insanity defense, 125–27
interrogation, 62–64, 71–72, 73, 75–76, 243, 245–46

judgment, 69–70, 79, 245
juveniles, 75, 90–92, 99, 239, 248

law school, 219–21, 222–24, 228–31, 233–34, 269–71
libel, 214, 216, 268
lie detector, 69–72
limited capacity, 156

marijuana, 32–33, 39, 111–12, 237
mens rea, 110
minors, 39, 47–49, 50–51, 90, 92, 105, 113, 156–59, 164, 208, 211, 213, 240
Miranda rights/warnings, 61–63, 78, 83, 243

negligence, 94, 109, 110–11, 113, 160–61, 203–204, 206, 207–209, 212, 252–53, 265
no-liability clause, 160

oral sex, 50–52, 54, 241
ordinance, 23–25, 37, 235

pre-nup (prenuptial agreement), 177–80, 262–63
presumption of paternity, 181–82
probable cause, 65–67, 244
promissory estoppel, 154–55, 260
prostitution, 51, 56–58, 242–43
public defender, 135–38, 139, 257–58

reasonable belief, 65, 68
reckless endangerment, 117
restitution, 88, 203

self-representation, 129–31
Sixth Amendment, 251, 256, 257
slander, 214–16, 268
speedy trial, 107–109, 251–52
statutory rape, 47–50, 112, 240

taxable income, 189–91, 263–64
tax law, 187, 233
tort, 29, 54, 203–16, 222, 266
trespassing, 112, 195, 198–99, 207–209, 266–67

unconscionability, 164–65, 167

warrants, 31, 77–80, 83, 246
wrongful arrest, 82

About the Authors

MICHAEL CICCHINI is a criminal defense attorney. *Super Lawyers* and *Milwaukee Magazine* have named him among "the top young lawyers" for 2006, 2007, 2008, and 2009. He has also published extensively on criminal and constitutional law—including articles in the *Tennessee Law Review* and the *Arizona State Law Journal*—and has been cited numerous times by other authors. He earned his JD, summa cum laude, from Marquette University Law School, and also holds an MBA degree and a CPA certificate. More information, including the full text of his published articles, can be found at www.cicchinilaw.com.

AMY KUSHNER is a lecturer in English at the University of Wisconsin–Parkside. She is also a contributing author to: *101 Horror Films*, *101 Science Fiction Films*, *101 Gangster Films*, and *101 War Films*, all published by the Barron's Educational Series. She earned her PhD in English Literature from Stony Brook University, and her BA, summa cum laude, from the University of Michigan, where she was named as a lifetime member of Phi Beta Kappa.